Britannica Student Encyclopedia

Volume 13

ENCYCLOPÆDIA
Britannica®

Chicago • London • New Delhi • Paris • Seoul • Sydney • Taipei • Tokyo

2010 Britannica Student Encyclopedia

Copyright © 2010 by Encyclopædia Britannica, Inc.

Library of Congress Control Number: 2009904642
International Standard Book Number: 978-1-61535-321-7

Printed at World Color Press in Versailles, Kentucky, U.S.A.
1st Printing, January 2010

Britannica may be accessed at http://www.britannica.com on the Internet.

The Taj Mahal is covered in white marble and gemstones.

(*See* Taj Mahal.)

A tapir has a soft, flexible snout like a short elephant trunk. It also has hoofed feet like those of a horse.

(*See* Tapir.)

People first drank tea as a kind of medicine.

(*See* Tea.)

Tigers live in the wild in China, Russia, and the southern parts of Asia.

(*See* Tiger.)

In 1985 deep-sea explorers found the remains of the *Titanic* near the Canadian island of Newfoundland.

(*See* Titanic.)

Tutankhamen became a ruler of ancient Egypt as a child.

(*See* Tutankhamen.)

Taft, William Howard

William Howard Taft was the 27th president of the United States.

William Howard Taft was president of the United States from 1909 to 1913. He later served as chief justice of the U.S. Supreme Court. He is the only person to have held the country's two highest offices.

Early Life

William Howard Taft was born into a wealthy family on September 15, 1857, in Cincinnati, Ohio. His parents were Alphonso Taft and Louisa Maria Torrey. His father was secretary of war and attorney general under President Ulysses S. Grant.

Taft graduated from Yale University in 1878 and Cincinnati Law School in 1880. He married Helen (Nellie) Herron in 1886. They had three children.

In 1887 Taft became a judge of the superior court of Ohio. He was named a judge of a U.S. circuit court in 1892.

Political Career

In 1900 President William McKinley asked Taft to organize a government for the Philippines. The country had come under U.S. control after the Spanish-American War of 1898. In 1901 Taft became governor of the Philippines. Taft returned home in 1904 to serve as secre-

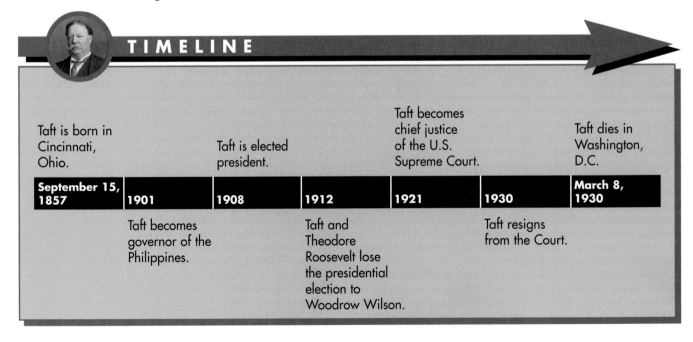

TIMELINE

Taft is born in Cincinnati, Ohio.

Taft is elected president.

Taft becomes chief justice of the U.S. Supreme Court.

Taft dies in Washington, D.C.

| September 15, 1857 | 1901 | 1908 | 1912 | 1921 | 1930 | March 8, 1930 |

Taft becomes governor of the Philippines.

Taft and Theodore Roosevelt lose the presidential election to Woodrow Wilson.

Taft resigns from the Court.

tary of war under President Theodore Roosevelt.

Presidency

Roosevelt supported Taft in the presidential election of 1908. He believed that Taft would continue his reforms. A Republican, Taft defeated the Democrat William Jennings Bryan to become president.

As president, Taft failed to solve the growing split between conservative and progressive Republicans. The progressives wanted Taft to continue Roosevelt's reforms. Taft did continue to attack the big business groups known as trusts. However, Taft disappointed progressives by approving a high tariff, or tax on imports. He also refused to hire progressives as his advisers.

Roosevelt and the progressives soon left the Republican Party to form the Progressive Party. In the 1912 presidential election the Republican Taft ran against the Progressive Roosevelt and the Democrat Woodrow Wilson. The split in the Republican Party allowed Wilson to win the election.

Later Years

After leaving office Taft taught law at Yale University. In 1921 President Warren G. Harding appointed Taft chief justice of the U.S. Supreme Court. Taft was happier in this post than he was as president. He helped the Court to work faster and to focus on the most important national cases.

Suffering from heart disease, Taft resigned on February 3, 1930. He died on March 8 in Washington, D.C.

▶ More to explore

Harding, Warren G. • Philippines • Roosevelt, Theodore • United States • United States Government

Taiga

The taiga is one of the major biomes of the world. Biomes are regions with similar climates and plants and animals. The main feature of the taiga is its conifer forests. Conifers are trees that form seeds inside cones. The taiga grows across the northern parts of Europe, Asia, and North America. Another name for taiga is boreal forest.

Features

In addition to its forests the taiga is known for its long, cold, snowy winters and short, cool summers. It lies just south of the cold, treeless area called the tundra. Where the two regions meet, there are few trees. The forests are

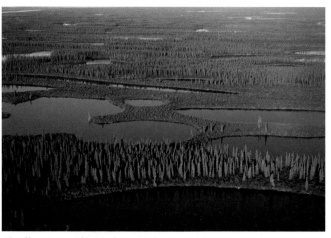

Shallow ponds and cone-bearing trees are common sights in the taiga.

thicker in the southern taiga. Many lakes and bogs are found in the taiga.

Life in the Taiga

The main trees of the taiga are conifers with needle-shaped leaves. In the south, trees with broad leaves—for example, alders, aspens, and birches—grow among the conifers. Mosses, liverworts, and lichens grow on tree trunks, rocks, and the ground.

The conifers in the taiga have features that help them to survive in the cold, snowy climate. Their branches point downward. This helps snow to slide off easily and keeps the branches from breaking off. In addition, conifers are a dark green color. This means they have more of the substance that allows green plants to soak in sunlight. They need to absorb as much sunlight as possible during the short summer.

Mammals in the taiga include lynx, wolves, moose, reindeer, beavers, shrews, voles, squirrels, and martens. Many birds come to the taiga in summer. Only a few types, including ravens and chickadees, stay through the long winter.

Resources

People cut down many of the trees of the taiga for wood. The earth under certain areas of the taiga is rich in petroleum (oil), natural gas, and coal. However, logging, oil drilling, and mining have harmed the environment in many parts of the taiga.

▶ **More to explore**
Biome • Conifer • Forest • Tundra

Did You Know?

Few cold-blooded animals, such as snakes, live in the taiga because of the low temperatures.

Tail

A young opossum hangs from a branch by its tail.

Many animals have a tail, which is a body part that extends from the hindquarters, or rear of the body. In animals that have a backbone, the tail is an extension of the backbone. This type of tail contains bones. In animals without a backbone, the tail does not contain bones.

The tails of most animals have one or more uses. Tails help many animals to move. Some types of monkeys use their tail to grab branches as they swing through the trees. A squirrel uses its tail to balance and steer as it leaps through the air. The tip of a mole's tail is very sensitive. This helps it to move backward through tunnels quickly. The tails of lobsters, fishes, and whales push them through water.

Some animals use their tails as weapons. Crocodiles and alligators swing their heavy, strong tails at enemies. A porcupine has sharp quills, or needles, at the end of its tail. A ring-tailed lemur marks its bushy tail with a bad-smelling odor and then waves it at other lemurs. A scorpion stings enemies or prey with its tail.

Many animals use their tails to communicate with other animals. A rattlesnake shakes its tail as a warning when it feels threatened. A male peacock displays his long tail feathers to attract females. This display shows the female how strong and healthy the male is.

▶ **More to explore**
Animal

Taino

▶ *see* Arawak.

Taipei

Population
(2008 estimate), city, 2,629,270; urban area, 6,698,320

Taipei is the capital of Taiwan, an island off the southeast coast of China. Taiwan is a province of China. However, Taiwan elects its own government to rule the island. Taipei is Taiwan's largest city. It is also the island's center of business, industry, and culture.

The 2-28 Peace Park is a popular place to visit in Taipei, Taiwan. It was named to honor a group of people who made a protest against their government on February 28, 1947.

Service industries such as banking, trade, and transportation are important to Taipei's economy. Many businesses in the city involve computers or other high-technology goods and services. Factories in Taipei make such products as electronics, software, cloth, and chemicals.

People from the Chinese mainland founded Taipei in the early 1700s. In 1886 China made Taiwan a province with Taipei as its capital. Japan ruled the island from 1895 to 1945. Taipei remained the capital during that period.

The Nationalist political party controlled mainland China in the early 1900s. In 1949 Chinese Communists took over the mainland. The Nationalists fled to Taiwan. They made Taipei their capital. The Nationalists and the Communists each claimed to be the true government of China. However, in 1971 the United Nations began treating the Communist mainland government as the only government of China.

Taipei grew greatly in the late 20th century. Many people now live in a relatively small city area.

▶ **More to explore**
China • Taiwan

Taiwan

Taiwan is a small island off the southeast coast of China. Taiwan is a province of China, not an independent country. However, Taiwan's government has the power to rule the island. Taiwan also calls itself the Republic of China. The capital is Taipei.

Geography
Taiwan lies in the Pacific Ocean about 100 miles (160 kilometers) from mainland China. The Philippines is to the south. Japan lies to the northeast.

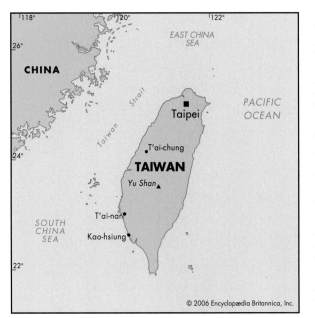

© 2006 Encyclopædia Britannica, Inc.

Mountains and hills cover the eastern two thirds of Taiwan. Low plains make up the western third of the island. The weather is warm and humid. Severe storms called typhoons often strike the island during the summer.

Plants and Animals
Thick forests cover much of Taiwan. Cyprus, cedar, juniper, maple, and pine trees grow in the mountains. Palm trees, bamboo shoots, and tropical evergreens grow in the lowlands.

Taiwan's animals include foxes, deer, wild boars, monkeys, and goats. The native Formosan black bear lives only in the mountains.

People
Nearly all the people in Taiwan are Chinese. Most of the Chinese have roots in southeastern China. They are often called the Taiwanese. A smaller group of Chinese came to Taiwan in 1949. Their descendants are called "mainlanders." The original people of Taiwan form only a tiny group. They live mostly in the mountains.

Mandarin Chinese is the main language. Taiwan's major religions are Buddhism and Daoism. Most people also follow traditional Chinese religions. Most of the population lives in cities and towns in the west.

Economy
Taiwan has a strong economy based on manufacturing and services such as banking. Factories make electronics,

A huge statue of the Buddha overlooks many other Buddha sculptures at a religious center in Taiwan. Many people in Taiwan practice Buddhism. Buddhism is a religion based on the teachings of the Buddha.

cement, iron and steel, cloth, chemicals, cars, and other goods.

Farmers in Taiwan grow rice, sugarcane, citrus fruits, bananas, and other crops. Fish, pigs, and chickens are other sources of food.

History
People from other Pacific islands and Asia first came to Taiwan between 12,000 and 15,000 years ago. Portuguese sailors arrived in 1590 and gave the island the name of Formosa. Dutch traders later took control of the island.

Chinese and Japanese Rule
In 1661 armies for the Ming Dynasty, or royal family, of China pushed out the Dutch. The Qing Dynasty of China took over in 1683. The Qing Dynasty ruled Taiwan for the next two centuries. Many Chinese people settled in Taiwan during this time.

In 1894–95 Japan and China fought each other in the Sino-Japanese War. At the end of the war, Japan took control of Taiwan. During World War II (1939–45) the Japanese used Taiwan as a military base. Taiwan returned to China's control in 1945.

Nationalist Government
In the late 1940s two groups, the Communists and the Nationalists, fought for control of China. In 1949 the Communists won. The Nationalists fled to Taiwan and set up their government there. Both the Communists and the Nationalists claimed to be the true government of all of China.

The United Nations (UN) treated Taiwan's government as the government of China until 1971. That year the UN accepted the mainland Communist government as the only Chinese government.

Taiwan Today
Taiwan held its first free elections in the 1990s. The Nationalists lost control of the government in 2000. A party called the Democratic Progressives took power. Meanwhile, some people began calling for complete independence from China.

▶ **More to explore**
China • Taipei

Did You Know?

The full Portuguese name of Taiwan—Ilha Formosa—means "Beautiful Island."

Tajikistan

The small country of Tajikistan lies in the heart of central Asia. Tajikistan's capital is Dushanbe.

Geography

Tajikistan shares borders with Uzbekistan, Kyrgyzstan, China, and Afghanistan. Almost all the land is mountainous. Tajikistan has a dry climate with hot summers and cold winters.

Plants and Animals

Grasses, bushes, and shrubs are the most common plants. Tajikistan's animals include great gray lizards, gophers, deer, tigers, jackals, and brown bears.

People

The Tajik people make up most of the population. The Uzbeks form the second largest group. The country's other peoples include Russians and Kyrgyz. Most of the people speak Tajik and practice Islam. Most Tajiks live in small villages along canals or rivers.

Many rugged, snow-covered peaks lie in the Pamir Mountains of Tajikistan.

Economy

Tajikistan is a poor country. Most people are farmers. The main crops are cotton, potatoes, wheat, tomatoes, and grapes. People also raise sheep, goats, and cattle. Tajikistan's factories produce aluminum, cloth, electricity, food products, machinery, and chemicals.

History

The Tajiks lived in the area by about 2,500 years ago. They set up states along the Silk Road, a trade route to China.

In the AD 600s and 700s Muslim Arabs conquered the area. Beginning in 999, many other groups ruled the land for hundreds of years.

Russia took control in the 1800s. In the 1920s Tajikistan became part of the Soviet Union. Tajikistan gained independence in 1991.

▶ **More to explore**
Dushanbe

Facts About
TAJIKISTAN

Population
(2008 estimate)
6,839,000

Area
55,300 sq mi
(143,100 sq km)

Capital
Dushanbe

Form of government
Republic

Major cities
Dushanbe, Khujand, Kulyab, Kurgan-Tyube

Taj Mahal

The Taj Mahal is considered one of the most beautiful buildings in the world. It is located in the city of Agra in northern India. A ruler named Shah Jahan had the Taj Mahal built as a monument and tomb for his beloved wife, Mumtaz Mahal.

Shah Jahan was the Muslim ruler of the Mughal Empire in India from 1628 to 1658. His wife died in 1631, and the construction of the Taj Mahal began the following year.

The monument is located on the bank of the Yamuna (or Jumna) River. It is surrounded by formal gardens and reflecting ponds. The building rests on a square marble base that rises 23 feet (7 meters) high. The building is roughly square-shaped. Each of the four faces of the structure has a large arch that rises 108 feet (33 meters) high. Above the center of the building is an onion-shaped dome.

Pure white marble covers the outside of the building. Set into the marble are gemstones of various colors. These include lapis lazuli, jade, crystal, turquoise, and amethyst. The stones form geometric and floral designs.

The interior of the Taj Mahal is a large room that contains monuments to Jahan and his wife. A carved marble screen surrounds these monuments. Beneath the monuments lie the actual tombs of Jahan and his wife.

White marble and gemstones cover the outside of the Taj Mahal. Some 20,000 people worked on the monument, which took 22 years to build.

Over the years the Taj Mahal has been affected by pollution from nearby factories as well as from motor vehicles. However, steps are being taken to prevent further damage to the site.

Tallahassee

ATLANTIC OCEAN

★ Tallahassee

Gulf of Mexico

Population
(2000 census)
150,624;
(2007 estimate)
168,979

Tallahassee is the capital of the U.S. state of Florida. The city lies on a series of rolling hills.

Many people in Tallahassee work for the government or in services such as health

Cypress trees grow from beneath the waters of Lake Bradford, in Tallahassee, Florida.

care or education. The city is home to Florida State University and other schools of higher learning. Tallahassee is also the trade center for crops and dairy products produced on nearby farms. Factories in the city make electronics and other products.

Tallahassee was originally an Apalachee Indian village. The village was already established by the time the Spanish explorer Hernando de Soto visited the area in 1539. Creek Indians later moved to Tallahassee. The U.S. government forced the Indians to leave the area in the early 1800s. In 1824 Tallahassee became the capital of the Florida Territory. Florida became a U.S. state in 1845. Tallahassee then became the state capital.

▶ **More to explore**
Florida

Tallchief, Maria

Maria Tallchief was one of the greatest U.S. ballerinas. She danced with the

New York City Ballet for 18 years. There she performed many dances created by George Balanchine, an important ballet director.

Tallchief was born on January 24, 1925, in Fairfax, Oklahoma, a town on an Osage Indian reservation. Her father was Osage. She began dancing at a young age. In 1942 she joined the Ballet Russe de Monte Carlo. In 1946 she married Balanchine, the company's choreographer, or dance arranger. The couple soon moved to New York City. There Balanchine founded what later became the New York City Ballet. With that company Tallchief became known for her performances in *The Firebird* and *The Nutcracker*. For one season she was the prima ballerina, or lead dancer.

Tallchief retired as a dancer in 1965. She then taught ballet and directed the Lyric Opera Ballet in Chicago. In 1980

Maria Tallchief was a famous ballerina. She was known for her fine ballet technique.

Tallchief and her sister, who was also a dancer, founded the Chicago City Ballet. The company lasted until 1987.

▶ **More to explore**
Ballet • Dance

Tallinn

Population
(2007 estimate)
396,850

Tallinn is the capital of Estonia, a country in northeastern Europe. Tallinn has a port on the Baltic Sea. It is Estonia's largest city.

Eastern Orthodox Christians worship at the Alexander Nevsky Cathedral in Tallinn, Estonia.

Tallinn's economy is based mainly on engineering, banking, trade, and other services. The shipment of goods through the port also brings money to the city. Factories in Tallinn make electronic equipment, machinery, cloth, and food products.

People settled in the Tallinn area in ancient times. The town was established by the 1100s. It suffered many invasions. It was ruled by Denmark, by German knights, and then by Sweden. Russia took control of all of Estonia in the early 1700s. In 1918 Estonia became an independent country with Tallinn as its capital.

In 1940 Estonia was forced to become part of the Soviet Union. For a time during World War II (1939–45), Germany controlled Tallinn.

Estonia became an independent country again in 1991. Tallinn remained its capital.

▶ **More to explore**
Estonia

Talmud

The Talmud is a collection of ancient Jewish teachings. The written laws of Judaism are found in the Torah, the first five books of the Hebrew Bible. People in ancient Israel also followed many oral, or unwritten, teachings. Jewish leaders, called rabbis, eventually wrote down those oral laws and traditions. They also added their own comments. These included interpretations of the laws as

Young men study the Talmud at a special school called a yeshiva. The Talmud is a collection of ancient Jewish teachings.

well as stories that helped explain moral lessons. Together, these collections of laws, interpretations, and stories are known as the Talmud.

The Talmud was written by many rabbis over hundreds of years. The first part of the Talmud is the Mishna, which states the oral laws. Scholars think that a rabbi in Palestine (a region of the Middle East) finished the Mishna in the early 200s. It has six sections, for laws on daily prayer and farming, special rituals, marriage, criminal and civil law, rules of the temple, and cleanliness.

The second part of the Talmud is the Gemara, which contains comments on the ideas in the Mishna. Rabbis wrote the Gemara from the 200s through the 500s. There are two versions of the Gemara—one written in Palestine and

one written in Babylonia (a historic region of southwestern Asia). Modern scholars consider the Babylonian version to be more complete.

▶ **More to explore**
Bible • Judaism • Palestine • Torah

Talon

▶ *see* Nail and Claw.

Tanganyika, Lake

Lake Tanganyika is the longest freshwater lake in the world and the second deepest. It is located in eastern Africa. The lake forms the border between Tanzania and the Democratic Republic of the Congo.

The lake is 410 miles (660 kilometers) long. It has a depth of 4,710 feet (1,436 meters). Many rivers flow into the lake. The largest are the Malagarasi, the Ruzizi, and the Kalambo. The lake's only outlet is the Lukuga River.

Rice and other crops are grown along the lake's shore. People also fish in its waters. Several important ports are found along the lake.

In 1858 Lake Tanganyika was first visited by Europeans. At that time British explorers were searching for the source of the Nile River.

▶ **More to explore**
Lake

Tanzania

Ngorongoro Crater is a popular tourist spot in Tanzania. Visitors to the area can see zebras and many other animals.

The country of Tanzania contains Africa's highest mountain and its largest lake. Dar es Salaam is the capital, but Tanzania's government has moved some of its offices to a new capital, Dodoma.

Geography

Tanzania has a coast on the Indian Ocean in the east. The country includes the mainland (called Tanganyika) and the islands of Zanzibar, Pemba, and Mafia. Tanzania shares borders with Kenya, Uganda, Rwanda, Burundi, the Democratic Republic of the Congo, Zambia, Malawi, and Mozambique.

Large plains, mountains, valleys, and lakes cover Tanzania's land. The great Serengeti Plain lies in the northeast. East of this plain is Mount Kilimanjaro, the highest point in Africa. Africa's huge Western Rift and Great Rift valleys run through the country. Along Tanzania's borders are three large lakes: Lake Nyasa,

Lake Tanganyika, and Lake Victoria. Lake Victoria is the world's second largest freshwater lake. (Lake Superior in North America is the largest.)

Most of Tanzania is hot and dry. The coast and the islands receive the most rain.

Plants and Animals

Forests grow in the rainy high areas. Grasslands and scattered trees cover much of the country. The large Serengeti National Park protects huge herds of wildebeests, gazelles, and zebras. The park also has many lions, leopards, hippopotamuses, giraffes, and baboons. Rhinoceroses and elephants survive in smaller numbers. Bands of chimpanzees live in the west.

People

Tanzania has more than 120 different ethnic groups. The Sukuma are the

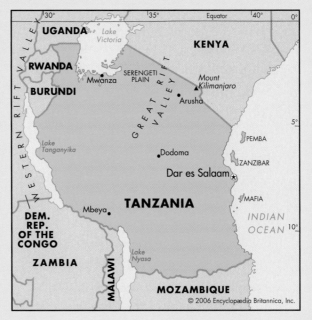

The Masai people live in Tanzania and neighboring Kenya. They are nomads, meaning that they usually do not live in permanent settlements. They follow their herds of cattle and other animals throughout the year.

country's largest group. The Sukuma and other groups have their own languages. Most Tanzanians also speak Swahili, which different groups use to communicate with each other. Some Tanzanians also speak English. The country's main religions are Christianity and Islam. Many people follow traditional African beliefs. Most Tanzanians live in small villages or in the countryside.

Economy

Tanzania's economy depends on agriculture. The main food crops are cassava, corn, sorghum, bananas, rice, and sweet potatoes. Farmers also grow coffee, cotton, cashew nuts, tea, and tobacco. Cloves are grown on the islands of Zanzibar and Pemba.

Small industries in Tanzania make food products, cement, clothing, beer, and cigarettes. Mines provide gold, diamonds, and gems, including tanzanites.

Facts About TANZANIA

Indian Ocean

Population
(2008 estimate)
40,213,000

Area
364,901 sq mi
(945,090 sq km)

Capital
Dar es Salaam
(acting)

Form of government
Republic

Major cities
Dar es Salaam, Arusha, Mbeya, Mwanza

History

Remains of some of the earliest known human ancestors have been found in Tanzania. Some are about 1.75 million years old. Groups of hunter-gatherers lived in the area as early as 5000 BC. Farmers and herders appeared around 1000 BC.

Arab and European Control

By AD 100 Arabs set up trading settlements on the East African coast. In the late 1400s the Portuguese arrived. About 200 years later the Arab rulers of Oman (a country on the Arabian Peninsula) gained control. More Europeans began arriving in the 1800s. Great Britain took over Zanzibar in 1890.

Germany took over the mainland in 1885. The land that is now Tanzania, Rwanda, Burundi, and part of Mozambique became known as German East Africa. In 1919, after World War I, Britain took control of the Tanzania portion. The British named the land Tanganyika.

Independence

Tanganyika gained independence in 1961, and Zanzibar became independent in 1963. The two joined to form the United Republic of Tanzania in 1964. Beginning in the 1990s hundreds of thousands of people poured into Tanzania to escape violence in neighboring countries.

▶ **More to explore**

Dar es Salaam • Kilimanjaro, Mount

Taoism

▶ *see* Daoism.

Tapir

A tapir walks along a riverbank in Ecuador.

Tapirs are mammals that live in swamps and in forests near rivers. They are related to horses and rhinoceroses. Three kinds of tapir live in Central and South America. Another kind lives in Southeast Asia.

A tapir has a heavy body with short legs. It has a soft, flexible snout like a short elephant trunk. Its feet have hooves, like those of a horse. Tapirs weigh 500 to 600 pounds (225 to 270 kilograms). They are 6 to 8 feet (1.8 to 2.4 meters) long, plus a short tail. They stand about 3 feet (1 meter) tall at the shoulder. The tapirs of the Americas have brown or gray hair. The tapir of Asia is black with some white parts.

Tapirs are shy animals that like the deep forest. They sleep most of the day. At night they come out to eat grass, leaves,

water plants, and fruit. A tapir uses its nose to move things aside and find food, like a horse does. Tapirs swim to escape their enemies, such as jaguars and tigers.

Tapirs are endangered, which means they are in danger of dying out. People hunt tapirs for food and sport. Plus, people have destroyed tapirs' homes by cutting down forests for wood.

▶ **More to explore**
Horse • Mammal • Rhinoceros

Tarsier

Tarsiers are tiny animals with huge eyes. Their excellent senses of sight and hearing make them good nocturnal, or nighttime, hunters. Tarsiers belong to

A tarsier has pads on the tips of its long fingers and toes. The pads are like suction cups. They help the animal cling to a tree trunk.

the group of animals called primates. Other primates include lemurs, monkeys, and humans. There are at least three different species, or types, of tarsier.

Tarsiers live in the rain forests of Indonesia and the Philippines. They spend most of their time in trees and can leap between trunks 10 feet (3 meters) apart.

Tarsiers have brown, gray, or reddish fur. They are only about 6 inches (15 centimeters) long with a thin, 10-inch (25-centimeter) tail. Tarsiers have a round head with large eyes and ears. Like an owl, a tarsier can turn its head halfway around. Tarsiers' fingers and toes have pads like suction cups that help them to grip branches.

Tarsiers sleep in trees during the day and hunt on the ground at night. They jump on their prey and grab it with their hands. Tarsiers eat small animals such as insects, lizards, and snakes. They do not eat plants.

Some tarsiers live alone. Others live in male and female pairs. They can have babies at any time of the year. The female is pregnant for six months and then gives birth to one offspring. A baby tarsier can climb and jump after only a few days. Tarsiers can live for about 12 years.

▶ **More to explore**
Lemur • Monkey • Primate • Rain Forest

Did You Know?

Tarsiers are the only primates that do not eat plants.

Tashkent

Population
(2007 estimate)
1,959,190

Tashkent is the capital of the country of Uzbekistan. It is one of the largest cities in central Asia. It is also a major center of culture and industry.

Many cotton farms surround Tashkent. Factories in the city make cotton cloth and machines used to process the cotton. Other factories make airplanes, packaged foods, and chemicals. Many people in the city work in government or business offices.

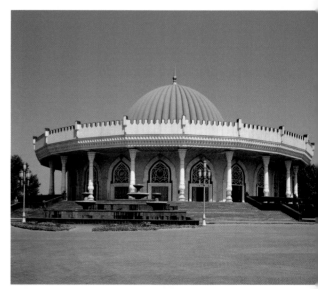

A museum in Tashkent, Uzbekistan, has a domed roof. It is named after Timur, a Mongol leader who ruled what is now Uzbekistan in the 1300s.

Tashkent dates back at least 2,000 years. In ancient times it was an important trading center. Many different groups, including the Turks, the Arabs, and the Mongols, ruled Tashkent over its long history.

In 1865 Tashkent became part of Russia. It soon became a regional capital. Along with Russia, the city became part of the Soviet Union in the early 1900s.

An earthquake destroyed much of Tashkent in 1966. The city was later rebuilt.

Uzbekistan became an independent country in 1991. Tashkent was made its capital.

▶ **More to explore**
Uzbekistan

Tasmania

Tasmania is the smallest state of Australia. Most of its land is a triangle-shaped island. The state also includes the nearby islands of Bruny, King, and Flinders as well as many smaller islands. Macquarie Island, about 900 miles

Tasmania, Australia, is home to small, fierce animals called Tasmanian devils. The island has many kinds of animals and plants that are found nowhere else on Earth.

(1,450 kilometers) to the southeast, is a part of Tasmania, too. Tasmania's capital is Hobart.

Geography

Tasmania lies about 150 miles (240 kilometers) south of Victoria, a state in southeastern Australia. The main island is 180 miles (290 kilometers) long. Its widest part is 175 miles (280 kilometers) wide. The state covers an area of 26,410 square miles (68,401 square kilometers).

A flat, raised area called a plateau covers much of the main island. Mountains rise in the west. Mount Ossa, at 5,305 feet (1,617 meters), is the highest point. The Derwent and the South Esk are the major rivers. The island also has more than 4,000 lakes. Most of these lakes are shallow. But Lake Saint Clair, with a depth of more than 700 feet (215 meters), is Australia's deepest lake. Tasmania's climate is mild and moist.

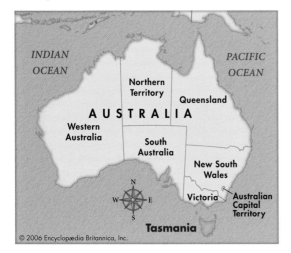

People

Tasmania is home to about 500,000 people. Most of them have British ancestors. Most of the people live in the southeast and the north. Hobart, in the southeast, is the largest city and main port. Launceston is the main city of northern Tasmania.

Economy

Many Tasmanians work in services—for example, communications, computer work, and tourism. Manufacturing is also important to the economy. Tasmania has many resources to use in manufacturing. Its forests provide wood for the lumber and paper industries. Mines provide iron, zinc, lead, copper, and tin, which are used to make metal products. In addition, Tasmania produces many foods and drinks. Tasmanian farmers grow potatoes, onions, peas, apples, grapes, and hops. They raise dairy cows, beef cattle, and sheep. The coastal waters provide fish.

History

Tasmanian Aborigines, or the first people in Tasmania, may have lived on the island as early as 40,000 years ago. The Dutch explorer Abel Tasman reached the island in 1642. He named it Van Diemen's Land after the governorgeneral of the Dutch East Indies (now Indonesia). At that time several thousand Tasmanian Aborigines lived on the island. The last full-blooded Tasmanian Aborigine died in 1876.

Tasmania became a part of the British colony of New South Wales (in

Port Arthur was a prison settlement in Tasmania, Australia, during the 1800s. Many convicts were taken there to work as punishment for their crimes. Today Port Arthur's buildings are in ruins. Many tourists visit them.

southeastern Australia) in 1803. In 1825 it became a separate colony. Many of the Europeans who lived there were prisoners sent to the island from Great Britain.

In 1856 the people of Van Diemen's Land elected their own government. They changed the island's name to Tasmania, after the explorer Tasman. In 1901 Tasmania became a state of Australia.

▶ More to explore
Australia • New South Wales • Victoria

Tax

Governments can get money in various ways. For example, they can charge fees for such things as driver's licenses. But almost every government gets money simply by demanding a certain amount from its citizens. Money collected in this way is called a tax.

Did You Know?

Tasmania is home to a unique animal called the Tasmanian devil. It was named for its fierce growl and bad temper.

Purposes of Taxes

Governments collect taxes for several purposes. The most important purpose is to get money to pay for government services. These services include protection by an army or police, road building, and public education. Some governments use taxes to change people's behavior. For example, they may put high taxes on tobacco to get people to stop smoking. Finally, governments may raise or lower taxes to help their country's overall economy.

Types of Taxes

There are many different types of taxes. Among them are income taxes, property taxes, and sales taxes.

A tax on the money that people make is called a personal income tax. Companies in the United States withhold, or hold back, a part of almost every worker's pay. They send this money to the U.S. government. After the end of the year, people send in income tax returns, which are forms that tell the government how much money they made. Some people then have to pay still more money, while others get back some of their money in a refund. Sometimes governments make rich people pay higher taxes than poor people. Companies also pay taxes on the money they make. This tax is called corporate income tax.

Taxes on the value of land, buildings, and some large possessions (cars, for example) are called property taxes. In the United States, state and local governments collect property taxes.

Some taxes are used to build and to take care of such public areas as parks and roads.

When people buy goods and services, they often pay a sales tax on top of the price. Sales tax is usually a certain percentage of the selling price. In the United States, each state has its own sales taxes. However, many countries have national sales taxes. European countries use a form of sales tax called a value-added tax (VAT).

History

In ancient times, most people gave goods or services to a ruler instead of taxes. A farmer might give part of his crop. An ancient Egyptian might help to build a pyramid. However, the rulers of ancient Rome collected taxes in the form of money.

Taxes grew in importance over the years, although people were often unhappy when governments demanded them. The colonists who started the American Revolution in 1775 were angry because they had to pay taxes to Great Britain without having votes in Parliament (the British legislature). An unfair tax system was also one of the

In the Boston Tea Party of 1773, some American colonists destroyed tea to protest a British tax.

causes of the French Revolution, which began in 1789.

In the 1900s some state governments in the United States and governments of other countries looked for ways to collect money without raising taxes. Many began using lotteries (gambling games) to raise extra money.

▶ **More to explore**
Economics • Government • Money

Taylor, Zachary

A hero of the Mexican War, Zachary Taylor was elected the 12th president of the United States in 1848. He died after only 16 months in office.

Early Life
Zachary Taylor was born on November 24, 1784, in Montebello, Virginia. His parents, Richard Taylor and Mary Strother, came from important Virginia families. Zachary grew up on a plantation in what is now Kentucky. There were no schools nearby, so he learned from a tutor.

In 1810 Taylor married Margaret Mackall Smith. They had six children.

Military Career
Taylor joined the Army in 1806. Over the next 40 years he became a respected military leader. His strength and courage earned him the nickname Old Rough and Ready. Taylor commanded troops in the War of 1812 and against Native Americans in various battles.

In 1846, just before the Mexican War, Taylor defended the border of Texas against Mexican troops. Taylor's troops defeated the Mexicans in two battles. After the United States declared war, Taylor crossed into Mexico and captured the city of Monterrey. In 1847 Taylor's forces defeated a larger Mexican army in

Zachary Taylor was the 12th president of the United States.

TIMELINE

Taylor is born in Montebello, Virginia.

November 24, 1784

Taylor joins the Army.

1806

Taylor leads troops in the War of 1812.

1812

Taylor defeats a Mexican army in the Mexican War.

1847

Taylor is elected president.

1848

Taylor fights the spread of slavery.

1849

Taylor dies in Washington, D.C.; Millard Fillmore becomes president.

July 9, 1850

the battle of Buena Vista. That victory made Taylor a national hero.

Presidency

The Whig Party chose Taylor to run for president in 1848. He defeated the Democratic candidate, Lewis Cass, in the election. Taylor was the first man to become president without any experience in politics.

President Taylor had to deal with the difficult issue of slavery. Although he owned slaves, Taylor opposed the spread of slavery. In 1849 he recommended that California be admitted to the Union as a free state—one that would not allow slavery. Taylor's recommendation angered proslavery Southerners in Congress.

Taylor did not live to see the Compromise of 1850, which temporarily settled the slavery crisis. On July 4, 1850, he became ill with cholera. He died on

July 9 in Washington, D.C. Vice President Millard Fillmore became president.

▶ More to explore

Fillmore, Millard • Mexican War • Slavery • United States • War of 1812

Tbilisi

Population
(2006 estimate)
1,103,300

Tbilisi is the capital of Georgia, a small country in the Caucasus Mountains of Asia. The city lies on the Kura River. It is Georgia's largest city by far. It is also a major center of industry, culture, and research.

Shops in Tbilisi, Georgia, use both the Georgian alphabet and the Latin alphabet for their signs.

Factories in Tbilisi make machinery, clothing, processed foods, and drinks. Many people in the city work for the government or in tourism or other service industries. Tourists often visit Tbilisi to bathe in the natural hot springs, where hot mineral water spouts from the ground.

Tbilisi was founded in the 450s. The city lay along an important trade route between east and west. This made Tbilisi a valuable prize for many conquering groups. Over the centuries it was ruled by the Persians, Byzantines, Arabs, and Mongols.

In 1801 Russia captured Tbilisi. It became the capital of the Russian province of Georgia. The Soviet Union made Georgia one of its republics in 1921. In 1991 Georgia became an independent country with Tbilisi as its capital.

▶ **More to explore**
Georgia, Republic of

Tea

Tea is a strong and energizing drink. It is made by soaking the leaves of the tea plant in hot water. Tea is especially popular in Asia, the United Kingdom, many former British colonies, and the Middle East.

The most common types of tea are black and green, both of which are made from the same plant. The plant likely grew first in China. It now also grows in many other parts of Asia, especially India. Countries in eastern Europe, Africa, and South America also grow tea.

Some teas have added scents or flavors, such as jasmine or orange. Although

Workers pick tea leaves in Malaysia.

most people drink their tea hot, many people in the United States drink iced tea. Other hot drinks made with plant leaves, flowers, or roots may also be called tea. Examples include chamomile tea, South American maté, and South African *rooibos*, or red tea.

According to legend, people first drank tea in China in about 2700 BC. At first people used tea as medicine. In about the AD 200s it became a daily drink. The Dutch and the English brought tea from China to Europe in the 1600s. From there it spread to Europe's colonies.

Technology and Invention

Technology is the use of knowledge to invent new devices or tools. Throughout history, technology has made people's lives easier.

Ancient Technology

Early humans set themselves apart from other animals when they learned to control fire. About 2 million years ago, they also learned to use stones as weapons or tools. This began a period that is known as the Stone Age. Stone Age people also learned to make pottery from clay.

Later on, people learned to work with metal. The people of Anatolia (now in Turkey) made copper tools and weapons as early as 6500 BC. In about 3000 BC people discovered that mixing copper with tin formed a stronger

Thousands of years ago Stone Age people learned to create tools and weapons by chipping away at pieces of stone.

metal—bronze. This discovery began the Bronze Age.

Two important developments took place in the Middle East at the beginning of the Bronze Age. One was the invention of the ox-drawn plow. The other was the invention of the wheel and axle. Many scientists date the beginning of civilization, or advanced culture, to this time.

In the 1000s BC the Hittite people of Anatolia learned to work with iron, which is stronger than bronze. This began the Iron Age. Eventually, people throughout Europe, Asia, and northern Africa made strong iron tools and weapons.

Technology in the Middle Ages

A period called the Middle Ages began in Europe in about AD 500 and lasted until about 1500. Many advances during this time came from other places—

for example, China, the Byzantine Empire, Persia, India, and the Islamic world.

By about the 1400s, Europeans learned the Chinese technique of casting iron. This involved heating iron in a special furnace and then pouring it into a mold to harden. Chinese inventors also developed black powder, the original form of gunpowder.

New sources of power were developed during this time. The horse became a major energy source with the invention of the padded horse collar. The collar meant that the horse could be used to pull plows and other objects. People also harnessed water and wind power to run new types of water mills and windmills.

Two kinds of technology helped to end the Middle Ages and to begin modern times. The rudder (a part for steering a ship), the triangular sail, and the com-

A French book from the late 1200s shows two important inventions: the windmill and the waterwheel. These devices use the power of the wind or the water to run machines, often to grind grain. Before they were invented, the labor of people or animals powered the machines.

pass made possible the sea voyages of European explorers. In about 1450 Johannes Gutenberg invented the printing press. As a result books could be produced in great numbers. Many people learned to read, and learning became widespread.

Industrial Revolution

Iron, Coal, and Steam

Early in the 1700s two English inventors set the stage for the Industrial Revolution. This was a period of great growth of industry. Abraham Darby discovered that a coke-burning furnace produced good iron. Coke is a form of coal. Thomas Newcomen invented a pump that kept coal mines from filling with water. A steam engine powered the pump.

With these developments, coal and iron production expanded rapidly. Iron remained the main metal for building and toolmaking until the late 1800s. At that time steel (a mixture of iron and carbon) began to replace regular iron.

Meanwhile, in the late 1700s steam began to replace wind and water as the major source of power. In a steam engine, burning coal heated water. The boiling water produced the steam that ran the engine.

Machines and Factories

Other inventions also sped up the production of goods—especially textiles, or cloth. By the early 1800s such machines as the power loom made cloth faster and easier to weave. Cloth making moved from homes and workshops into large mills and factories. The factories used steam engines to run many of their machines. Other industries followed this model.

Transportation

Between 1765 and 1782 James Watt of Scotland greatly improved the steam engine. John Fitch of the United States ran a steamboat as early as 1787. In 1803 Richard Trevithick created the steam locomotive.

In 1856 Henry Bessemer of England invented an improved way of making steel. People began using steel to build railroads, ships, and bridges. (People also used steel to build the first skyscrapers.)

In 1876 the German engineer Nikolaus August Otto built a gasoline-powered engine. By 1885 two Germans named Gottlieb Daimler and Karl Benz had used gasoline engines in the first successful automobiles.

Electricity

In the first half of the 1800s scientists learned to generate, or produce, electricity. In 1835 Samuel F.B. Morse of the United States used electricity in his telegraph. This invention allowed people to communicate across long distances. In 1876 the U.S. inventor Alexander Graham Bell invented the telephone, which also used electricity. Thomas Edison demonstrated the electric lightbulb in 1879. Electric power also came to be used for electric railways in cities.

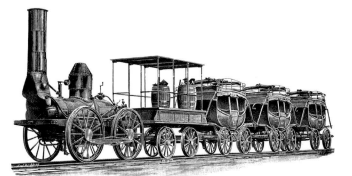

A steam locomotive called the Dewitt Clinton hauled carriages on railroad tracks in the early 1830s.

Petroleum and Chemicals

In the second half of the 1800s petroleum, or oil, became a major power source. Edwin Laurentine Drake drilled the first successful oil well in the United States in 1859. Petroleum can be made into gasoline, fuel oil, and many other products.

In 1856 William Henry Perkin of England made a breakthrough in the

Thomas Alva Edison holds up an early version of the electric lightbulb, which he developed in the late 1800s.

field of chemistry. Starting with coal tar, which is made from coal, he invented the first synthetic, or artificial, dye. Coal tar and petroleum proved to be useful in the making of drugs and plastics as well.

Modern Technology

Mass Production

Modern manufacturing methods can produce goods in large numbers. This is called mass production. An important technique of mass production is the assembly line. An assembly line product is put together one piece at a time as it moves past workers on a conveyor. Each worker does just one task. In the early 1900s Henry Ford perfected the assembly line to make automobiles in the United States.

Later in the 1900s robots began to replace assembly-line workers. A robot is a machine that operates on its own.

A machine in a factory produces polyester cloth. Polyester is an artificial fiber made from coal and petroleum (oil) products.

Air and Space

In 1903 the Wright brothers of Ohio produced the first successful airplane. The Russian-born inventor Igor Sikorsky developed the helicopter in the United States in the 1930s. At about the same time Frank Whittle of England developed a jet engine for airplanes.

German scientists used rockets in World War II (1939–45). Rocket engines carry oxygen as well as fuel. This allows them to work in outer space, where there is no oxygen. After the war the Soviet Union and the United States developed programs to send people into outer space in space ships. In 1957 the Soviets put the first artificial satellite into orbit around Earth. The Americans landed the first human on the Moon in 1969.

Energy

Beginning in the 1900s scientists found ways to harness the energy of sunlight. Solar furnaces use mirrors to focus solar heat. Solar cells make electricity from sunlight.

Scientists also found ways to use the energy that holds atoms together. Atoms are the tiny units that make up everything. This energy is called nuclear energy. It found its first use in very powerful bombs called atom bombs that the United States used in World War II. Scientists soon learned to use nuclear energy to make electric power.

Electronics and Computers

Electronic products changed people's lives greatly during the 1900s. Electronic products rely on electricity to carry or process information. Radios were some of the first electronic products. By the 1920s radio programs were being broadcast into people's homes. Television, a later electronic product, came into use during the 1930s and 1940s. The first electronic computers were invented in the 1940s as well.

Later in the 1900s electronic products became smaller. People discovered how to fit the parts that make electronic products work onto tiny chips called integrated circuits. These chips made personal computers possible. Other inventions of the late 1900s also used integrated circuits. They included compact disc players, cellular telephones, digital cameras, and many other electronic products.

Technology and Medicine
In the 1900s scientists began applying technology directly to living things. Scientists developed electrical devices to help people with disabilities. Some devices, such as hearing aids and kidney dialysis machines, operate from outside the body. Doctors place other electrical devices inside the body. For example, pacemakers help keep hearts beating steadily.

In addition, scientists learned how to cut and rejoin genes. (Genes are tiny units within cells that carry information about a living thing.) This is called genetic engineering. Genetic engineering may help to cure human diseases. It also

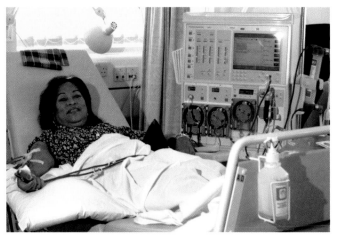

A dialysis machine helps a patient whose kidneys are not working properly. The machine does the work that the kidneys would do. Blood from the patient flows through the machine, where it is cleaned. The blood then returns to the patient's bloodstream.

helps to produce food plants that resist diseases.

▶ More to explore
Airplane • Automobile • Bridge • Bronze Age • Computer • Electricity • Electronics • Genetics • Industrial Revolution • Iron Age • Nuclear Energy • Petroleum • Plastic • Printing • Radio • Railroad • Robot • Rocket • Ship • Steel • Stone Age • Telephone • Television • Textile

Tecumseh

Tecumseh was a leader of the Shawnee Indians. He fought to keep American settlers out of the Ohio River valley.

Tecumseh was born in 1768 in what is now Ohio. His father was a Shawnee chief. His mother belonged to the Creek tribe. When Tecumseh was about

Tecumseh led American Indians in a losing struggle to keep their land.

6 years old, his father was killed in a battle with white settlers. Then Tecumseh's mother returned to her people. An older sister and brother raised Tecumseh. A Shawnee chief later adopted him.

Tecumseh spent his life fighting American settlers who were taking land from Indians. As a boy during the American Revolution, he helped the British attack American colonists. Later he united Indian tribes to fight Americans. He worked with his brother Tenskwatawa, a religious leader.

Tecumseh saw the War of 1812 as a chance for his people to recover the land they had lost. The war was between Great Britain and the United States. Tecumseh and his warriors helped the British. They hoped a British victory would allow the Indians to take back their land.

British and Indian forces captured Detroit, Michigan. Later Tecumseh's army invaded Ohio with the British. After failing to capture a fort near Toledo, they crossed into Canada. The British and the Indians were defeated near the Thames River in Ontario on October 5, 1813. Tecumseh was killed in the battle.

▶ **More to explore**
Shawnee • War of 1812

Teeth

Many vertebrates, or animals with backbones, have teeth inside their mouths. Teeth are hard, bony structures that grow from the jawbone. Humans and other animals use their teeth to bite and to chew food.

Types of Teeth
Teeth of different shapes do different jobs. Front teeth, called incisors, bite and cut. Pointed teeth, called cuspids or canines, tear and shred. Teeth with two points, called bicuspids, tear and grind. Back teeth, called molars, crush and grind.

Humans have two sets of teeth during their lives. The first set consists of 20 teeth. These are called primary, or baby, teeth. When a child is about 6 years old, these teeth begin to loosen and fall out. Over the next eight years 28 permanent teeth replace all the baby teeth. When a person is around age 20, four more

Age 6

permanent teeth □ primary teeth ▨

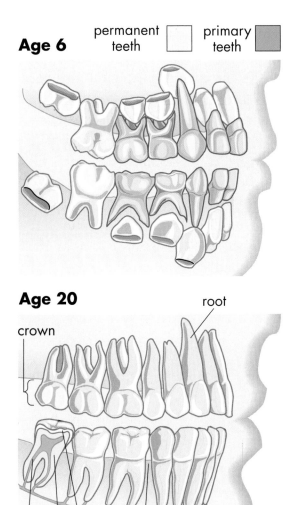

Age 20

crown

root

pulp   enamel   gum   nerves and blood vessels

dentin

Inside View

A diagram shows the teeth of people at two different ages. Humans have two sets of teeth during their lives. The first set is called the primary teeth. At about age 6, one's primary teeth begin to fall out. The second set, called the permanent teeth, replaces them.

molars, called wisdom teeth, grow in. Many people have their wisdom teeth removed to keep their other teeth straight.

Tooth Structure

The visible part of a tooth is called the crown. Several layers make up the crown. The outer layer is a hard white covering called enamel. Enamel protects the tooth from wear and tear. Below the enamel is dentin. This yellow, bonelike material is softer than enamel. Dentin makes up the largest part of the tooth.

The center of a tooth is called the pulp. The pulp is soft tissue that contains blood and nerves. Nerves in the teeth send signals to the brain about heat, cold, or pain.

The soft tissue around the base of each tooth is called the gum. The roots of the teeth lie below the gums. A tooth has between one and three roots. A gluelike substance called cementum coats the roots. Cementum keeps the teeth stuck in the jawbone.

Problems with Teeth

A common problem with teeth is tooth decay, or cavities. Cavities can form if a sticky film called plaque is allowed to build up on the teeth. Germs in plaque eat away the tooth and cause pain and infection. Dentists fill cavities to prevent further damage. Plaque can also make gums red, sore, and weak. Over time, weakened gums can wear down so far that the teeth fall out. People can keep teeth healthy by brushing and flossing teeth and visiting the dentist.

Sometimes the teeth do not bite together properly. Dentists called orthodontists can straighten teeth.

▶ **More to explore**
Dentistry • Mouth

Did You Know?

The tusks of elephants and walruses are enlarged upper teeth.

Tegucigalpa

Population
(2007 estimate)
944,400

Tegucigalpa is the capital of Honduras, a country in Central America. The city lies on the Choluteca River. It is located in a hilly region surrounded by mountains. It is the largest city in Honduras.

Tegucigalpa is one of the main industrial centers in Honduras. Factories in the city make cloth, clothing, processed foods such as sugar, and other goods.

The Honduras region was once part of a Spanish colony. Spanish conquerors founded Tegucigalpa in 1578. They built the city as a center for mining silver from the nearby mountains.

Many houses sit on hilly ground in Tegucigalpa, Honduras.

Honduras became an independent country in 1838. For much of the 1800s the country's capital shifted back and forth between Tegucigalpa and the city of Comayagua. Tegucigalpa became the permanent capital of Honduras in 1880.

A strong hurricane hit Honduras in 1998. Tegucigalpa was severely damaged.

▶ **More to explore**
Honduras

Tehran

Population
(2007 estimate)
7,873,000

Tehran is the capital of Iran, a country in the Middle East. The city lies in the Elburz Mountains. It is Iran's largest city by far. It is also a center of education and industry.

Factories in Tehran make such products as cloth, cement, food products, and medicines. A factory near the city processes oil. Many people in Tehran work in government offices.

Iran has a long history. For most of that history Tehran was not a very important city. In ancient times the city of Rayy

The bazaar is the market district of Tehran, Iran. The merchants there offer many types of goods for sale.

was the capital of Iran. Tehran was a suburb of Rayy. Invaders nearly destroyed Rayy in 1220. Many people from Rayy then moved to Tehran.

Tehran was the home of several of Iran's rulers from the 1500s to the 1700s. It became the capital of Iran in the 1780s. Since then it has been the country's most important city. In the early 1900s Iran's rulers made Tehran larger and more modern.

During a revolution in 1979 Islamic leaders took control of Iran. Supporters of the revolution captured the U.S. embassy in Tehran. They held a group of Americans as hostages there from 1979 until 1981.

In the 1980s a long war between Iran and Iraq hurt Tehran's economy and development. In the 1990s the city began to grow again.

▶ **More to explore**
Iran

Tel Aviv–Yafo

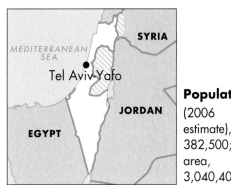

Population
(2006 estimate), city, 382,500; urban area, 3,040,400

Tel Aviv–Yafo is a large city in Israel, a country in the Middle East. It is Israel's main center of business and culture. The city lies on the Mediterranean Sea. As its name suggests, it was created by combining two towns: Tel Aviv and Yafo. Yafo is the Hebrew name for the ancient port city of Jaffa.

Most of Israel's banks and insurance companies have headquarters in Tel Aviv–Yafo. Many people in the city work in business services, tourism, and trade. Factories in Tel Aviv–Yafo process diamonds and foods and make clothing, medicines, and high-technology products.

Tel Aviv–Yafo is a modern city on the shore of the Mediterranean Sea.

Many thousands of years ago Jaffa was a city of the Canaanite people. It was later ruled by the Egyptians, Israelites, Persians, and others. Muslim Arabs ruled Jaffa from about the 1200s to the middle of the 1900s.

Jewish settlers founded Tel Aviv in 1906. At first it was a suburb of Jaffa. At the time both cities were part of the land called Palestine. In 1948 part of Palestine, including Tel Aviv and Jaffa, became the country of Israel. Israel soon combined Tel Aviv and Jaffa to create the city of Tel Aviv–Yafo.

▶ **More to explore**
Israel

Telecommunication

Telecommunication is any kind of human communication that takes place across a distance. Several inventions have helped people to communicate quickly over great distances.

The first important step in telecommunication was the telegraph. It was invented in the 1830s by Samuel F.B. Morse. His invention could send coded messages instantly over a wire. Long and short electrical signals, called Morse Code, stood for letters of the alphabet. By 1866 telegraph cables under the Atlantic Ocean linked North America and Europe.

The telephone made it possible to send the sound of the human voice over a wire. Alexander Graham Bell invented the telephone in 1876. Today telephone signals may travel through wires, through fiber-optic cables, or even as radio waves.

In the 1890s Guglielmo Marconi invented the wireless telegraph, or radio. Like the telegraph, his invention sent messages in code, but the messages traveled through the air as radio waves. Spoken messages were first sent by radio in 1907. The first network of radio stations in the United States was the National Broadcasting Company (NBC). It broadcast its first radio programs in 1926.

By the 1930s it was possible to send a picture as well as a sound signal over radio waves. This was the beginning of television (TV). In 1936 the British Broadcasting Corporation (BBC) started the world's first TV programming. Now television signals may travel as radio waves or through cables.

Today the Internet makes it possible for people around the world to communi-

Short-wave, microwave, cellular telephone, and other types of telecommunication antennas receive and send messages from high ground near Phoenix, Arizona.

cate through computers. The U.S. government developed an early form of the Internet in the 1960s and 1970s. Telephone wires, television cables, fiber-optic cables, and satellites connect computers around the world to the Internet.

▶ **More to explore**
Communication • Internet • Radio • Telegraph • Telephone • Television

Telegraph

The telegraph is a device for communicating over a distance. It uses electricity to send coded messages through wires. In the middle of the 1800s the telegraph was the fastest way to communicate over long distances.

Invention of the Telegraph

The first two working telegraphs were invented at about the same time in the 1830s. In Great Britain two inventors built a telegraph that used six wires and five needles. A part called the transmitter sent electric currents through the wires. At the other end, the currents moved needles on a part called the receiver. The receiver had a special plate with letters and numbers on it. The needles pointed to the letters and numbers to spell out messages.

Meanwhile, in the United States, Samuel F.B. Morse worked on a telegraph of his own. Morse developed a new system for sending telegraph messages. It used dots, dashes, and spaces to stand for letters and numbers. This system is called Morse Code. Morse and his part-

The telegraph invented by Samuel F.B. Morse had a key for tapping out messages.

ner, Alfred Vail, built a telegraph with just one wire. The transmitter had an arm called a key. The person sending the message pressed the key to tap out messages in Morse Code.

In 1843 the U.S. government paid Morse to build the first long-distance telegraph line. It ran 35 miles (60 kilometers) from Washington, D.C., to Baltimore, Maryland. The next year Morse sent the first message through the system. The message was "What hath God wrought!"

The Telegraph Industry

Morse's telegraph started an entire industry. By the end of 1861 a telegraph line ran all the way across the United States. By the end of the 1800s telegraph lines crisscrossed the world. In the early 1900s a new kind of telegraph could print out messages. Later telegraphs could send messages through the air instead of through wires. The wireless telegraph was an early form of radio. By the end of the 20th century the telegraph had been mostly replaced by faster communications that used computers.

▶ **More to explore**
Electricity • Morse Code • Radio
• Telecommunication

Telephone

The telephone is a very common device for communicating over a distance. With a telephone, a person can talk almost instantly with someone on the other side of the world. Most telephones are linked to each other by wires. Others, such as cell phones, are connected by invisible radio waves that travel through the air.

How a Traditional Telephone Works

A traditional telephone depends on wires to send sound. It has a handset and a base that are connected by a cord. The handset is the part that a person holds to make or answer a call. One end of the handset has a microphone for talking. The other end has a small loudspeaker for listening. The base connects the telephone to an electric current through a wire.

When the caller speaks into a telephone, the microphone changes the sound of the person's voice into an electric signal. The base sends out the signal through its wire. How the signal travels from there depends on where the call is going. It can remain an electric current, passing through wires and cables. It can travel through thin glass fibers in the form of

light. This way of sending information is called fiber optics. Or the signal can be changed into radio waves and sent through the air by antennas and satellites. When the signal reaches the telephone at the other end, its loudspeaker changes it back into the sound of the caller's voice.

Cordless Telephones

A cordless telephone is more convenient than a traditional telephone. It does not have a cord connecting the handset and the base. It allows a person to walk around the house while talking.

A cordless telephone uses both electric signals and radio waves. The base receives the call as an electric signal, like a corded phone does. Then the base turns the electric signal into radio waves. Using an antenna, the base sends the waves through the air to the handset. The handset's antenna picks up the waves. Then the handset turns the waves back into sound.

Cell Phones

Cellular telephones, or cell phones, are even more convenient than cordless phones because they work over a much wider area. Because of this, in some places they are called mobile phones. They send and receive calls using radio waves.

Cell-phone companies divide up an area, such as a city, into sections called cells. Each cell has a tower for receiving and sending out radio waves. If a caller travels from one cell into another, the call switches from tower to tower. This means that a cell phone can work any-

Did You Know?

The word telephone comes from the Greek words *tele,* meaning "far" and *phone,* meaning "sound."

How a Phone Sends and Receives Sound

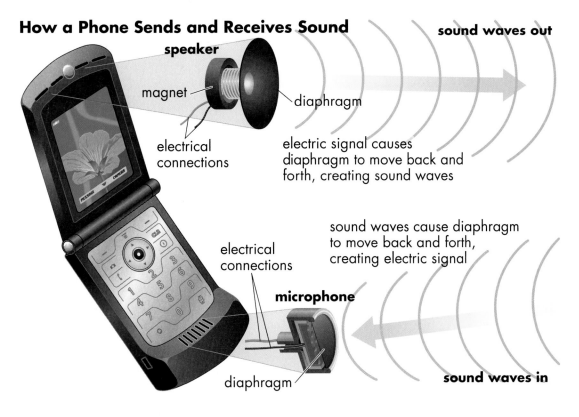

speaker

sound waves out

magnet

diaphragm

electrical connections

electric signal causes diaphragm to move back and forth, creating sound waves

sound waves cause diaphragm to move back and forth, creating electric signal

electrical connections

microphone

diaphragm

sound waves in

place that the cell-phone company's network reaches. Cell-phone networks can stretch across an entire country.

A cell phone sends out a special signal whenever it is turned on. The signal lets the network know where to send the calls that come to that phone.

Many cell phones can do things other than make calls. Certain kinds can get information from the Internet or send and receive e-mail. Some cell phones can take photographs.

History

Not everyone agrees who invented the telephone. However, Alexander Graham Bell usually gets the credit. In 1876 he sent the first words by telephone. Later that year Bell made the first long-distance call. He talked with his assistant, who was 2 miles (3.2 kilometers)

away. By 1915 people could place telephone calls across the United States. Telephone service across the Atlantic Ocean began in 1927. The first cell phones appeared in the late 1970s.

Telephones had no dials in the first part of the 1900s. Instead of dialing, callers told a telephone operator the number they wanted to call.

At about the same time advances in electronics made telephones useful for more than just talking. Fax machines became common in the 1970s. They use telephone wires to send words and pictures. Today many computers connect to the Internet through telephone lines.

▶ **More to explore**

Bell, Alexander Graham • Electricity • Fiber Optics • Radiation • Satellite • Sound • Telecommunication

Telescope

A telescope is an instrument that allows people to see distant objects. Telescopes are important tools in astronomy, or the study of planets, stars, and other objects in outer space. There are several different types of telescopes. Some, called light telescopes, gather light from objects. Other telescopes gather different kinds of information about the object being viewed.

Light Telescopes

There are two basic types of light telescopes: refracting telescopes and reflecting telescopes. A refracting telescope uses lenses. A lens is a curved piece of glass that refracts, or bends, light. A reflecting telescope uses mirrors. Some telescopes use both lenses and mirrors.

A refracting telescope is a tube with one or more lenses at each end. Light from a far-off object enters the far end of the tube. The lens or lenses at that end, called objective lenses, bend the light. They focus it at a point near the other

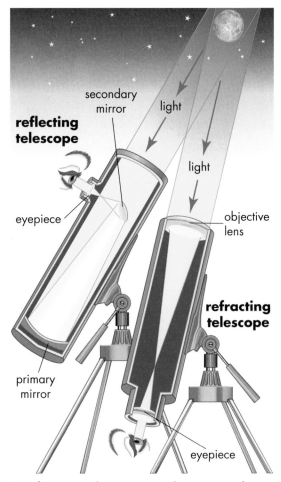

A refracting telescope uses lenses to enlarge an image. A reflecting telescope uses curved mirrors and sometimes lenses as well.

end of the tube. The light forms an image, or picture of the object, at this point. The lens or lenses at this end, called the eyepiece, magnify the image.

Reflecting telescopes are much more powerful than refracting telescopes. A reflecting telescope has a curved mirror at the bottom of the tube. Light from an object reflects, or bounces, off the mirror. The mirror focuses the light at a point in the tube. A second mirror sits in the way of this focused light. It sends the light out the side of the tube, through an eyepiece. A lens in the eyepiece magnifies the image formed by the light.

In some reflecting telescopes light passes though a lens before hitting the curved mirror. The lens helps to make the image sharper.

Some light telescopes are fairly small tubes that sit on a stand and can be carried around easily. Buildings called observatories house much larger, more powerful light telescopes. Spacecraft may also carry light telescopes. The Hubble Space Telescope, which orbits Earth on a spacecraft, is a type of reflecting telescope.

Other Telescopes

Some types of telescopes do not collect light. These telescopes collect other forms of energy from space—for example, radio waves, infrared radiation (a type of heat), and X-rays. Planets, stars, gas, and other things in space give off these types of energy.

Radio telescopes look like huge bowls. They collect radio waves that travel to Earth's surface. Infrared, X-ray, and other similar telescopes are mounted on spacecraft.

All these telescopes allow scientists to gather information about things in space that cannot necessarily be seen. For example, they have shown that there is water vapor in other parts of the Milky Way galaxy. They have also helped scientists understand how stars and planets form and how stars die.

History

By the early 1600s several people had made simple refracting telescopes. In

The Very Large Array is a group of 27 bowl-shaped radio antennas in the state of New Mexico. Each antenna is 82 feet (25 meters) across. When used together they make one very powerful radio telescope.

1609 the Italian scientist Galileo improved the design of a telescope made by a Dutch inventor. Later in the 1600s several inventors, including the English scientist Isaac Newton, built reflecting telescopes.

A U.S. astronomer built the first radio telescope in 1937. Other scientific telescopes developed along with spacecraft, which scientists began launching in the 1950s.

▶ **More to explore**
Astronomy • Galileo • Lens • Light • Mirror

Television

Television, or TV, is a system for sending moving pictures and sound from one place to another. It is one of the most important and popular forms of communication. TV programs provide news, information, and entertainment to people all over the world.

People who own plasma TVs often hang them on a wall. Plasma TVs are thinner and lighter than standard TVs.

How TV Works

TV begins with a television camera, or video camera. The camera records the pictures and sound of a TV program. It changes the pictures and sound into electric signals. A TV set receives the signals and turns them back into pictures and sound.

The TV Signal

A standard TV camera changes the pictures into an electric signal called the video signal. The video signal carries the pictures in the form of tiny dots called pixels. The camera's microphone changes the sound into another electric signal, called the audio signal. The video and audio signals together form the TV signal.

Digital TV, or DTV, is a newer way of handling TV signals. A digital TV signal carries pictures and sound as a number code, like a computer does. A digital signal can carry more information than a standard signal can, which creates better pictures and sound. High definition TV, or HDTV, is a high-quality form of digital TV.

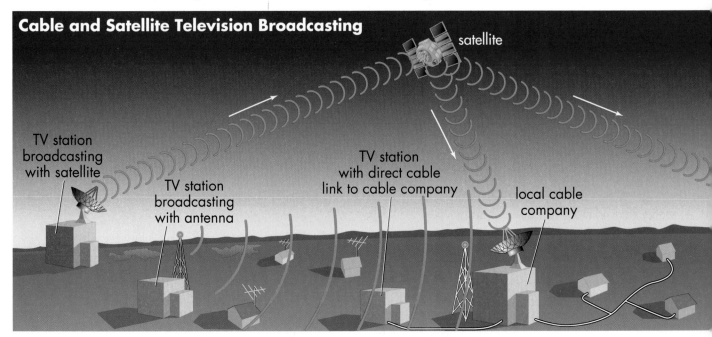

Cable and Satellite Television Broadcasting

satellite

TV station broadcasting with satellite

TV station broadcasting with antenna

TV station with direct cable link to cable company

local cable company

Television stations may broadcast, or send, TV signals with antennas, satellites, or cables. The signals sent with antennas may reach houses directly.

A TV signal can reach a TV set in several ways. Local TV stations use antennas to send, or broadcast, signals through the air as radio waves. Cable TV stations send signals through underground cables. Satellites, or spacecraft, traveling high above Earth can send signals to special antennas called satellite dishes. A signal can also come from a VCR, DVD player, or DVR (digital video recorder) connected to the TV set. VCRs, DVRs, and some DVD players can record a TV signal coming into the TV and then play it back later.

Display

A standard TV set turns the video signal into beams of tiny particles called electrons. It shoots these beams at the back of the screen through a picture tube. The beams "paint" the pixels on the screen in a series of rows to form the picture. The TV set sends the audio signal to loudspeakers.

LCD and plasma TVs form the picture differently. They do not use a picture tube and electron beams. Because they do not hold a picture tube, LCD and plasma TVs are much thinner and lighter than standard TVs. They can even hang on a wall.

LCD stands for liquid crystal display. Liquid crystal is a substance that flows like a liquid but has some tiny solid parts, too. The display sends light and electric current through the liquid crystal. The electric current causes the solid parts to move around. They block or let light through in a certain way to make the picture on the screen.

A plasma display has many tiny cells, or units, containing gas. Electricity sent through the gas forms a plasma. A plasma is a bunch of particles that have an electric charge. The plasma gives off light, which makes the picture.

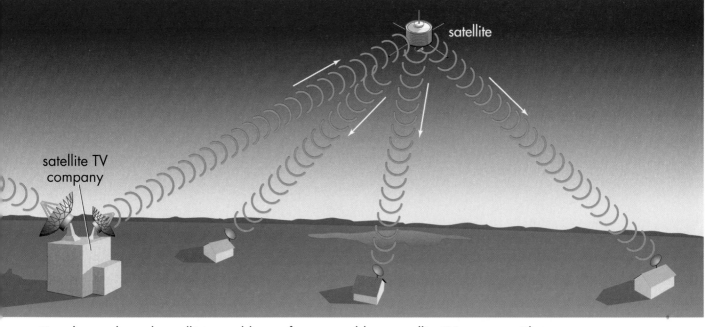

Signals sent through satellite or cables go first to a cable or satellite TV company. Those companies then send the signals to homes through other cables or satellites.

History

Inventors in Great Britain and the United States made the first demonstrations of TV in the 1920s. The first working TV sets appeared in the 1930s. In 1936 the British Broadcasting Corporation (BBC) started the world's first TV programming. The first commercial television stations in the United States started broadcasting in 1941.

Many families bought their first TV set after World War II, in the late 1940s and the 1950s. The first sets could show only black-and-white pictures. Color TV and cable TV started in the 1950s. Digital TV arrived in the 1990s.

▶ **More to explore**
Camera • Electronics • Radio • Telecommunication

Temple

A temple is a building that people use for worshipping gods or for other religious purposes. The houses of worship in many ancient religions were called temples. Hinduism, Buddhism, and several other religions today also have temples. The architecture of temples varies from place to place.

The temples of ancient Mesopotamia (in what is now Iraq) were highly decorated towers called ziggurats. They were shaped like pyramids with large steps. In ancient Egypt temples often had large, decorated columns. In the Americas the Inca and the Maya built pyramid-shaped temples.

The ancient Greeks and Romans built temples that have influenced architecture until the present day. A Greek temple was made of marble or stone. It had columns that enclosed a space holding an image of a god. An altar to that god stood outside the temple. Roman temples were similar, but the altar was inside the temple.

Hinduism and Buddhism began in ancient India. People there carved temples out of cliffs. Later Indian temples were freestanding. They often included tall, elaborately carved towers. Today Hindu and Buddhist temples throughout eastern Asia range from small and simple to huge and complex.

Other religions that have temples include Shinto and Jainism. Jewish synagogues are often called temples, too. Islamic temples are called mosques. Christian houses of worship generally are known as churches. However, Mormons (followers of the Church of Jesus Christ of Latter-day Saints) have temples for special religious ceremonies.

Buddhist monks walk past a Buddhist temple in Bangkok, Thailand.

▶ **More to explore**
Church • Mosque • Synagogue

Tennessee

The Great Smoky Mountains lie in the eastern part of Tennessee.

The name Tennessee comes from a Cherokee Indian word, Tanasi. Tanasi was the name of a major Cherokee village in the area. Tennessee is known as the Volunteer State. The nickname came from the large number of men who volunteered for military service in the War of 1812. The capital is Nashville.

Geography
Tennessee is located in the south-central part of the United States. It borders eight states. In the west the Mississippi River separates Tennessee from Missouri and Arkansas. Virginia and Kentucky lie to the north of Tennessee. Mississippi, Alabama, and Georgia are to the south. In the east Tennessee shares a border with North Carolina.

Eastern Tennessee lies within the Appalachian Mountain chain. The Blue Ridge Mountains along the Tennessee–North Carolina border include the range known as the Great Smoky Mountains. West of the mountains is an area of low ridges. The central part of the state is a region with generally flat but sometimes rolling land. Western Tennessee consists of plains, including a narrow strip of swamp and floodplain along the Mississippi River.

Tennessee has a moderate climate. Winters are cool and summers are warm.

People
Most of Tennessee's early white settlers came from the Eastern states. These people were mainly English, Scots-Irish, and German. Today about four fifths of the Tennessee population is white and of European heritage. African Americans are by far the largest minority group; they represent 16 percent of the state's population.

Economy
Manufacturing and service industries dominate Tennessee's economy. The state's factories produce motor vehicles

© 2006 Encyclopædia Britannica, Inc.

and parts, processed foods, chemicals, and many other products.

Leading service industries include health care, real estate, and tourism. Tourists visit Tennessee's natural wonders, such as the Great Smoky Mountains. Civil war battlefields and the musical attractions located in Memphis and Nashville are also popular. Tennessee's major agricultural products include cattle, chickens, greenhouse plants and produce, and dairy goods.

History

Native Americans including the Cherokee and the Chickasaw lived in the area that is now Tennessee before European settlers arrived. In the second half of the 1600s both the French and the English claimed the area. Settlers from both countries built forts and trading posts. In 1763 Britain took control of the whole area.

The first permanent white settlement in the region was started in 1769. Many other people from the American colonies followed. In 1796 Tennessee became the nation's 16th state.

The American Civil War (1861–65) divided Tennessee. The eastern part of the state sided with the North, but the western planters and slave owners supported the South. Tennessee battlefields at Shiloh and other places were sites of intense fighting during the war.

In 1933 the United States government created an agency called the Tennessee Valley Authority (TVA). Under the

TVA, new dams and hydroelectric power plants were built on Tennessee rivers. The dams and power plants helped control floods and generated electricity for the region.

Tennessee was a center of the civil rights movement in the 1950s and 1960s. Tragically, Memphis was the scene of the 1968 killing of civil rights leader Martin Luther King, Jr. In the 1990s the population of Tennessee increased faster than that of the United States as a whole. Tennessee's economy also grew during this period. The state supported this growth by encouraging the development of many different types of industry.

▶ **More to explore**
Cherokee • Nashville

The Cumberland River reflects the skyline of Nashville, the second largest city in Tennessee. The BellSouth Building is topped by two spires. It was the tallest building in the state when it was built in 1994.

Facts About TENNESSEE

Flag

Population
(2000 census)
5,689,283—
rank, 16th state;
(2008 estimate)
6,214,888—
rank, 17th state

Capital
Nashville

Area
42,143 sq mi
(109,151 sq km)—rank, 36th state

Statehood
June 1, 1796

Motto
Agriculture and Commerce

State bird
Mockingbird

State flower
Iris

Tennis

Tennis is a fast-paced sport for two or four players. It can be played either outdoors or indoors. Tennis players use a stringed racket to hit a ball over a net. They score points by hitting the ball out of the opponent's reach.

Court and Equipment

Tennis is played on a rectangular court. The court is 78 feet (23.8 meters) long. The width depends on whether there are two or four players. For a singles match (two players), the court is 27 feet (8.2 meters) wide. For a doubles match (four players), the court is 36 feet (11 meters) wide. The surface of the court may be grass, clay, or a hard material such as concrete. The court is divided in half by a net that is 3 feet (0.9 meter) high.

The only equipment needed for tennis is a racket and a ball. A tennis racket has a frame with crossed strings attached to it. Most racket frames are made of a light-weight material such as graphite. Tennis balls are small, light, and bouncy. They are usually yellow or white.

Playing the Game

A tennis game begins with a serve. One of the players, called the server, stands at one end of the court. The server throws the ball into the air and tries to hit it over the net. The opponent tries to return the serve—hit the ball back over the net. The players hit the ball back and forth until one of them fails to make a good return. Then the other player scores a point. The players try to hit the ball to a part of the court where the opponent will have a hard time returning it.

The serve is the most important stroke in tennis. The served ball must land in a boxed area on the opponent's side of the

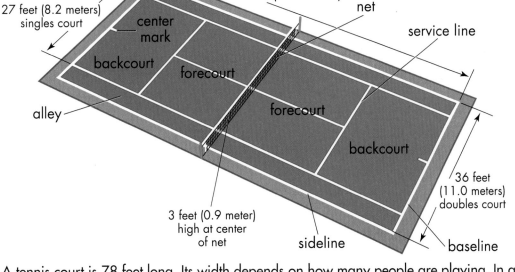

A tennis court is 78 feet long. Its width depends on how many people are playing. In a singles match, or a match for two players, the court does not include the alleys. The alleys are used only for doubles matches, in which four people play. The alleys make the court wider.

Doubles tennis is played with two players on a side. A doubles court is slightly wider than a singles court.

court. If the ball misses that box, it is called a fault. The server then gets another chance to serve. If the server makes another fault, the opponent gets a point. On the other hand, the server earns a point by serving the ball so well that the opponent cannot hit it. This is called an ace.

A player needs four points to win a game. Points are counted in four stages: 15 for the first point, 30 for the second, 40 for the third, and game. A score of zero is called love. The server's score is given first. For example, if the score is 30–love, the server has two points and the opponent none. If both players reach 40, the score is called deuce. The player who scores the first point after deuce must also get the next point to win the game. In other words, a player must win by two points.

A series of games makes up a set, and a series of sets makes up a match. The first player to win six games traditionally wins a set. But again, a player must win by two. This means that a player cannot win a set by a score of 6–5. The set con-

tinues until one player wins by two games—for example, 7–5 or 8–6. To win a match, a player usually has to win either two out of three or three out of five sets.

History

Major Walter Clopton Wingfield of Great Britain published the first book of tennis rules in 1873. The first tennis championship took place four years later. It was held in a part of London, England, called Wimbledon. Tennis reached the United States in the 1870s.

Four major international tennis tournaments take place each year—one in Australia, one in France, one in the United Kingdom, and one in the United States. A player who wins all four is said to have won the Grand Slam.

Tenzing Norgay

Tenzing Norgay was an expert mountain climber. In 1953 he and Edmund Hillary of New Zealand became the first people to set foot on top of Mount Everest, the world's tallest peak.

Tenzing Norgay was born on May 15, 1914, in Tshechu, Tibet. He was a Sherpa. Sherpas are people known for their strength and endurance at high altitudes. Tenzing worked on many Everest expeditions. On March 10, 1953, he began climbing with a group that included Hillary. The two men reached the top on May 29. Tenzing left a food offering, a common practice in his Buddhist religion. He died on May 9, 1986, in Darjeeling, India.

▶ **More to explore**
Everest, Mount • Hillary, Edmund

Teresa, Mother

The Roman Catholic nun called Mother Teresa received the Nobel peace prize in 1979 for helping to relieve the sufferings of the poor. She was especially active in the slums of Calcutta (now Kolkata), India.

She was born on August 27, 1910, in Skopje, Macedonia. Her birth name was Agnes Gonxha Bojaxhiu. In 1928 she joined a community of nuns in Ireland called the Sisters of Loretto. Weeks later she sailed to India. For the next 17 years she taught at a school in Calcutta run by the Sisters of Loretto.

In 1946 Mother Teresa decided to spend her life helping the sick and the poor. She studied nursing and started working in the slums. In 1948 she founded the Missionaries of Charity, a religious order of women dedicated to serving the poor. Mother Teresa led the order for nearly 50 years. It opened schools for children and centers to treat the blind, the disabled, the old, and the dying. She received many awards for her work.

In 1989 Mother Teresa suffered a heart attack. Despite her poor health, she continued to work in Calcutta most of the time until she retired in March 1997. She died there on September 5, 1997. After her death, the Missionaries of Charity carried on her work in more than 90 countries.

▶ **More to explore**
Roman Catholicism

Did You Know?

In 1963 the Indian government awarded Mother Teresa the title Padmashri ("Lord of the Lotus") for her services to the people of India.

Mother Teresa

Termite

Termites are insects that eat wood. They can damage buildings, furniture, and other wooden items. There are more than 1,500 species, or kinds, of termite. They are most common in tropical rain forests.

Termites build damp nests in wood or underground. Some underground nests rise partly above the ground as mounds or towers. The nests are made of dirt, clay, and chewed wood.

Termites live in organized groups called colonies. Each colony has three kinds of

Termites eat their way through a piece of wood.

termite: royalty, soldiers, and workers. Each kind of termite has a certain job within the colony.

The royalty is made up of a king and queen. They are responsible for reproduction. These termites have wings and eyes. A queen can grow to more than 4 inches (10 centimeters). Kings are smaller.

Once a year pairs of young kings and queens leave the nest. Each pair starts a new colony. Soon the young queens begin laying 3,000 to 5,000 eggs a day.

The soldiers and the workers are grayish white, blind, and wingless. They are usually less than 0.25 inch (1 centimeter) long. Soldiers guard the nest against enemies, mainly ants. Workers provide the colony with food.

Termites eat mostly wood. They attack and often destroy trees, fence posts, houses, and furniture. But termites also help nature by breaking down dead wood into nutrients. The nutrients can

then be recycled and used by bacteria and plants.

▶ **More to explore**
Insect • Nest

Terrorism

Terrorists are people who use fear to try to change society. They create fear by committing violent crimes. In the 21st century many countries consider terrorists to be more dangerous than enemy armies.

Goals

Not all terrorists want the same thing. Some want to overthrow a government. They are called revolutionary terrorists. Examples include the Red Brigades in Italy in the 1970s and the Shining Path in Peru in the 1980s and 1990s. Both groups wanted to establish Communist governments.

Other terrorists want independence for a particular group. In Sri Lanka a group called the Liberation Tigers seeks a homeland for the Tamil people. Several Palestinian groups want to start a Palestinian state in the Middle East and to weaken or destroy Israel.

Some terrorists oppose minority groups. The Ku Klux Klan (KKK) was formed in the United States in the 1860s to prevent African Americans from voting. Later the KKK also targeted Catholics, Jews, and other groups.

Sometimes the rulers of a country practice another kind of terrorism by killing their own citizens. Such rulers want to make people afraid to go against their power. Joseph Stalin of the Soviet Union and Saddam Hussein of Iraq ruled by terror.

Methods and Weapons

Terrorists often use bombs. They might carry bombs in cars, in packages, or on their bodies. They might also send bombs in packages. People called suicide bombers intend to die when they set off their explosives.

Terrorists can also release chemicals or other harmful substances. In 1995 a Japanese group released poison gas into the subway system in the city of Tokyo. Twelve people were killed. In 2001 five people died in the United States after someone mailed letters containing the disease anthrax.

Terrorists also kidnap or assassinate (murder) leaders. Or they might hijack, or seize, boats or airplanes. Sometimes they hold the passengers as hostages until their demands are met.

History

The word terrorism was first used in the French Revolution, which began in 1789. It described the way some of the revolutionary leaders punished those who opposed their actions.

In the late 1800s people called anarchists started to use terrorism. Anarchists want to do away with all government. An anarchist killed U.S. President William McKinley in 1901.

Terrorists crashed an airplane into the Pentagon, near Washington, D.C., on September 11, 2001. The Pentagon is the headquarters of the U.S. Department of Defense.

Anarchists also killed several European leaders.

In the 1900s more groups used terrorism than ever before. One reason is that deadly weapons became easier to get. Another reason is that airplane travel gave terrorists new ways to commit violence. Many of the groups that used terrorism had political goals. Others had very strong religious beliefs.

In September 2001 members of a group called al-Qaeda hijacked four airplanes in the United States. They crashed three of them into buildings. Their targets included the World Trade Center in New York City and the Pentagon, near Washington, D.C. It was the deadliest terrorist act up to that time. About 3,000 people were killed. Soon afterward U.S. President George W. Bush declared a "war on terror."

▶ **More to explore**
Crime • Ku Klux Klan

Texas

Texas was an independent nation before becoming part of the United States. It had won freedom from Mexico in 1836. Nine years later on December 29, 1845, Texas was admitted to the Union. Its national flag then became its state flag. This red, white, and blue flag with a single star was the origin of the Texas nickname, the Lone Star State. Austin is the capital.

Geography

Texas is located in the south-central part of the United States. The river called the Rio Grande separates Texas from the country of Mexico on the southwest. The Gulf of Mexico lies to the south-

The Guadalupe Mountains National Park in western Texas features rugged mountains surrounded by a desert.

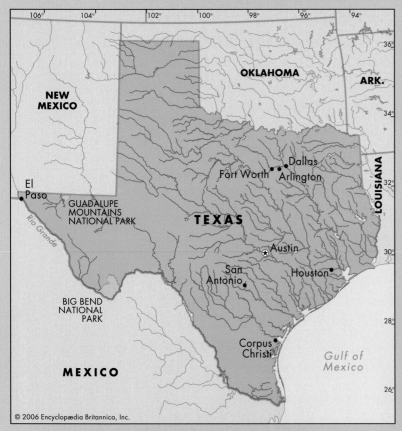

© 2006 Encyclopædia Britannica, Inc.

east. East of Texas are Louisiana and Arkansas. New Mexico is to the west, and Oklahoma is to the north.

The landscape of Texas consists mainly of plains and hills. The largest natural region is the coastal plain that covers southern and eastern Texas. It consists of flat, low prairies that stretch far inland from the Gulf of Mexico. In the central and west-central parts of the state are raised plateaus and hill country.

The Texas panhandle is a block of land that extends northward above the rest of the state. It is a flat, dry area with frequent sandstorms. The eastern edge of the panhandle and the north-central part of the state are lowland regions of prairie and rolling plains. The most rugged, mountainous land in Texas lies in the far west.

People

During the late 20th century Texas was one of the fastest-growing states in the country. Texas is now second in population only to California. Three of its urban centers—Houston, Dallas, and San Antonio—are ranked among the country's 10 most populated cities.

Whites of European heritage represent more than half of the state's residents. Hispanic Americans, mostly of Mexican origin, make up almost a third of the population. About 12 percent of the people are African American.

Economy

The Texas economy is among the largest in the country. Major parts of the economy include commercial trade, real estate, and finance. Tourism is also valuable to the state. About 40 million people visit the state each year.

The state's top manufacturing industries are in the field of high technology. These industries include the production of computers and electronic products. Texas is the home of Dell, a major computer company. Another company in the state, Texas Instruments, is a major producer of electronic goods and military equipment. Oil production and the manufacture of chemical and petroleum (oil) products also contribute to the state's economy.

In agriculture, Texas ranks first in the country in the production of cattle. Other valuable farm products include cotton and chickens.

History

Native Americans lived in the Texas region before Europeans arrived. Early tribes included the Caddo, the Jumano, and others. Later the Comanche moved into the area.

The Spanish began to explore the Texas region in the early 1500s. In 1685 the French explorer Sieur de La Salle started a settlement along the Texas coast. It did not last long, but it did make the Spanish move more quickly to build settlements of their own. San Antonio was founded in 1718 and became the main settlement of Spanish Texas.

Sand dunes stretch along an island off the coast of Texas in the Gulf of Mexico.

Facts About
TEXAS

Flag

Population
(2000 census)
20,851,820—
rank, 2nd state;
(2008 estimate)
24,326,974—
rank, 2nd state

Capital
Austin

Area
268,581 sq mi
(695,621 sq
km)—rank, 2nd
state

Statehood
December 29,
1845

Motto
Friendship

State bird
Mockingbird

State flower
Bluebonnet

When Mexico declared its independence from Spain in 1821, Texas became part of Mexico. During this period, Mexico allowed pioneers from the United States to enter the territory and set up colonies. Stephen F. Austin brought the first group of colonists to a site along the Brazos River. Austin is often called the Father of Texas.

Texans soon became unhappy with the Mexican government. In 1835 they revolted, and the next year they declared independence. In the most famous battle of the Texas war for independence, the Texans fought heroically to defend a mission called the Alamo. They lost at the Alamo, but they eventually defeated the Mexicans at a battle along the San Jacinto River. Texas became an independent republic in 1836. Sam Houston, the leader of the war, was elected its first president.

In 1845 Texas was admitted to the United States as the 28th state. Like other Southern states, Texas allowed slavery at that time. It joined the Confederacy during the American Civil War (1861–65). Although Texans fought for the South, the state itself was far removed from the major battlefields.

After the war Texas cowboys began driving cattle northward to markets or ranges. This vital industry led to the popular image of the cowboy in song, story, and film. The great cattle drives continued until about 1890.

The state's oil industry owes much to a place named Spindletop. Located near

Restaurants and cafés draw many people to the section of San Antonio, Texas, known as the River Walk.

Beaumont, Spindletop became the state's first great oil well in 1901. Numerous other wells followed. A huge oil field in eastern Texas was discovered in 1930.

On November 22, 1963, U.S. president John F. Kennedy was shot to death in Dallas. The vice president, Texas politician Lyndon B. Johnson, became the country's next president.

Another politician from Texas, George Bush, served as the country's president from 1989 to 1993. His son George W. Bush was elected president in 2000 and reelected in 2004. The Bushes were only the second father and son to both serve as president (the first were John Adams and John Quincy Adams).

▶ **More to explore**
Alamo • American Civil War • Austin

Textile

Merchants in the country of Uzbekistan display many kinds of colorful cloth for sale.

The word textile commonly means woven or knitted cloth. Lace, felt, and many other kinds of cloth are considered textiles, too. Even nets, rope, and yarn may be called textiles. People use textiles to make clothing, towels, sheets, table linens, carpets, boat sails, flags, and many other things.

Textile production is one of the world's major industries. Factories throughout the world produce many tons of textiles every year. But people still create textiles in small shops and at home as well.

Making Textiles

To create textiles, people first make thread or yarn out of fibers. Some fibers are natural—for example, cotton, wool, linen, and silk. Others are artificial, or man-made—for example, nylon and polyester. Then people weave, knit, knot, loop, or braid the thread or yarn together. These processes may be done by hand or by machine. People also may make textiles by pressing or gluing fibers together.

People often dye the thread or yarn before making it into textiles. They also may dye or print designs on cloth after it is made.

History

People have made yarn and woven cloth for thousands of years. Some of the world's oldest textiles have been found in ancient Egyptian tombs. Fragments of 3,000-year-old cloth also have been found in South America.

At first, people made cloth for themselves and their families. Eventually craftspeople took over the work and divided it into separate trades. Different workers spun the yarn, dyed it, and wove it into cloth. Other workers sold the cloth in shops. In the Middle Ages (about AD 500 to 1500) certain cities and regions became known for the kinds of textiles they made.

People made textiles by hand or with simple machines until the 1700s. Several inventions then made weaving faster. By the 1800s water and steam power ran many textile-making machines. Since that time, called the Industrial Revolution, textiles have been made mainly in factories.

▶ **More to explore**
Clothing • Fibers • Industrial Revolution

> **Did You Know?**
>
> Rayon was the first artificial textile fiber. It was first made in the 1800s.

Thailand

The local name for Thailand means "land of the free." True to its name, Thailand is the only country in Southeast Asia that was never ruled by European powers. Thailand's capital is Bangkok.

Geography

Thailand is shaped like an elephant's head. Narrow southern Thailand is the trunk, and the north is the head and the ear. Thailand shares borders with Myanmar, Laos, Cambodia, and Malaysia. The Andaman Sea, a part of the Indian Ocean, lies to the west. The Gulf of Thailand lies to the east.

Mountains and deep river valleys cover northern Thailand. The highest peak, Mount Inthanon, is 8,481 feet (2,585 meters) high. The mountains run down the western border into the south. The Chao Phraya is the country's major river. It flows through plains in central

An unusual rock formation stands in a bay in southern Thailand.

Thailand. The northeast is a broad, flat area called the Khorat Plateau.

Winds known as monsoons affect Thailand's climate. The winds bring a hot season, a rainy season, and a cool season.

Plants and Animals

Bamboo, coconut palms, mangroves, ferns, and mango and papaya trees grow in Thailand. Teak and other hardwood trees grow in the rain forests of the north.

Small numbers of wild elephants, rhinoceroses, and tapirs live in Thailand. Many monkeys and birds live in the forests. Lizards, frogs, snakes, and crocodiles are common.

People

Thai people make up most of the population. Chinese people form a smaller group. The country also has small

© 2006 Encyclopædia Britannica, Inc.

groups of Malays, Khmer, and others. Thai is the main language, but English is also widely spoken.

Almost all the people of Thailand follow Buddhism. Some people in the south, especially Malays, practice Islam. Most people live in rural areas.

Economy

Tourism is one of Thailand's largest industries. Manufacturing is another important part of the economy. Some of the major products are clothing, computers and other electronics, cement, sugar, and jewelry. Thailand is one of the world's largest producers of the metals tungsten and tin. The country's mines also provide coal, natural gas, and gems.

Many Thai people work in farming. The main crops include rice, sugarcane, cassava, and corn. Thailand also produces natural rubber, pineapples, and bananas. Pigs, chickens, and fish are other sources of food.

History

Thousands of years ago people in what is now Thailand grew rice and made metal tools. Between the AD 500s and 800s the Mon people set up small Buddhist kingdoms. By the 1100s the Khmer people of what is now Cambodia ruled parts of eastern Thailand.

Thai peoples moved into the area from China in about the 900s. In the 1200s they founded two kingdoms in what is now northern Thailand. The Sukhothai kingdom was founded after a local Thai ruler led a revolt against the Khmer. The

Tourists ride tame elephants in Thailand.

Lan Na kingdom was founded after another Thai ruler conquered a Mon kingdom.

In the 1300s the kingdom of Ayutthaya took the place of Sukhothai. The kingdom came to be known as Siam. Siam conquered Lan Na in the 1700s.

In 1782 a royal family called the Chakri dynasty came to power in Siam. During the 1800s Siam stayed independent while Europeans took over neighboring countries. In 1932 a military revolt ended the Chakri dynasty's absolute control over the country. Siam then became a constitutional monarchy. This means that the country still has a king from the Chakri dynasty, but his powers are limited. In 1939 the country became known as Thailand.

The military took control of Thailand in 1947. In 1973 students held protests that led to a more democratic government. But military leaders took power several times in the following years.

▶ **More to explore**
Bangkok • Buddhism

**Facts About
THAILAND**

Population
(2008 estimate)
64,316,000

Area
198,117 sq mi
(513,120 sq km)

Capital
Bangkok

**Form of
government**
Constitutional
monarchy

Major cities
Bangkok, Samut
Prakan, Non-
thaburi, Udon
Thani, Nakhon
Ratchasima

Thames River

© 2006 Encyclopædia Britannica, Inc.

The Thames River has been the main waterway of England since the time of the ancient Romans. Compared to the great rivers of the world, the Thames is neither long nor mighty. Its importance comes from the great civilization that arose on its banks.

The Thames begins in the Cotswold Hills of central England. From there it

There are many important buildings along the Thames River. The group of buildings at left is the Houses of Parliament, in London, England. This is where members of the British Parliament meet.

winds about 210 miles (338 kilometers) from west to east. After passing the city of Oxford, it flows through the countryside and then into London. The many landmarks along the Thames in London include the Houses of Parliament, Saint Paul's Cathedral, the Tower of London, and the Millennium Dome. The Thames empties into the North Sea.

People have lived in the Thames Valley for thousands of years. Before railways and good roads were built, the Thames was the area's main trade route. Over time many industries were set up along the banks. Today millions of people depend on the river for water and for sewage removal.

▶ **More to explore**
England • River

Thanksgiving

Thanksgiving is a yearly holiday marked by feasts and family gatherings. The day is celebrated in the United States, Canada, and other countries. It takes place on the fourth Thursday in November in the United States. In Canada it occurs on the second Monday in October. Both countries celebrate Thanksgiving with turkey feasts. In the United States, Thanksgiving Day parades and football games have become important traditions as well.

The Pilgrims of the Plymouth colony held the first Thanksgiving in 1621. They had landed in America on their ship the *Mayflower* in December 1620. Only half of them survived that first

A family prepares to eat a turkey dinner together at Thanksgiving.

winter. The next year, the harvest in the fall was good. To celebrate their harvest, the colonists and their Native American guests enjoyed a three-day feast.

Sarah Josepha Hale, the editor of a popular women's magazine, led the effort to have Thanksgiving become a national celebration in the United States. In 1846 she started sending letters to important politicians in order to achieve her goal. Finally, in 1863, President Abraham Lincoln proclaimed a national day of Thanksgiving. In December 1941 Congress officially named the fourth Thursday in November as Thanksgiving Day.

Theater

A theater is a place where people go to see plays and other performances. The word theater can also refer to everything involved in producing a live staged performance. The most common form of theater is a drama, or play. A drama is a story that is acted out for an audience.

Other kinds of theatrical productions may feature elements other than a story. They include musicals, puppet shows, circuses, operas, and ballets and other dance performances.

Inside the Theater

The part of a theater where the actors perform is called the stage. The most common kind, called a proscenium stage, is like a room with three walls. The audience sits in an auditorium and views the production as though looking through the fourth wall. Some theaters have a thrust stage, which extends partly into the seating area. The audience sits on three sides of the extended section of a thrust stage. In an arena stage the audience surrounds the stage. An arena stage is also called theater-in-the-round.

Other important parts of the theater include the backstage area and the dressing rooms. There is also a booth where technicians control the lighting and sound.

People in Theater

Many people work together to create theater. In a play actors have the most visible roles. The main people behind the scenes are the producer and the director. As the play's main businessperson, a producer obtains and manages all the money. The director decides how the play will be brought to life. This involves overseeing the actors and the behind-the-scenes crew. The director also runs rehearsals, or practices. A playwright writes the script, which contains the words the actors say.

Did You Know?

The word theater comes from a Greek word meaning "a place for seeing."

The stage manager oversees all behind-the-scenes activity during the production. The set designer creates backdrops and furniture. The property master manages the small items, or props, used onstage. Lighting experts focus light on the stage to concentrate on certain activity and to set a mood. The makeup artist and costume designer help the actors look their parts.

Other types of theatrical productions may involve other people with special talents. For example, in puppet theater various people design, make, and operate the puppets. In productions featuring dance a person called a choreographer may make up all the dance steps and movements. Musicians and composers may be a key part of productions that use music.

History

Early Theater

In ancient Greece plays were performed as part of special festivals. The audience sat on seats carved into the side of a hill overlooking the stage. Some ancient Greek theaters could seat as many as 20,000 people.

In Europe during the Middle Ages (AD 500–1500) plays were often related to Christianity. At first they were performed in churches. Later they were performed outdoors—on the church steps, on decorated platforms, or sometimes even in wagons.

In the 1300s a type of theater called Noh was developed in Japan. Noh plays combine words, music, and dance to portray legends. Men or boys play all the parts, including the female characters. The actors do not act out scenes. Instead they use their movements and appearance as symbols to suggest the story. A Noh play takes place on a thrust stage. The stage has four pillars topped by a curving temple roof.

The Renaissance (1300s to 1500s) was a period of great artistic creation in Europe. The large theaters built then set the pattern for today's theaters. Grand spectacles staged in these theaters were usually for the upper classes. The common people went to see groups of traveling actors perform comic entertainment outdoors.

In the late 1500s many theaters opened in London, England. The most famous was the Globe Theater, where William Shakespeare staged many of his plays. The Globe had a thrust stage that extended halfway into an open court-

In the 1600s many of William Shakespeare's plays were performed at the Globe Theater in London, England. The theater was torn down in the mid-1600s, but it was rebuilt on almost the same spot in the 1990s.

yard. The common people stood in the courtyard. Wealthier members of the audience sat in seats. During Shakespeare's time women did not perform in plays. The female characters were played by men or boys who dressed as women.

Modern Theater

In Japan in the 1600s a new form of drama called Kabuki appeared. It focused on singing, dancing, and mime (movement without words). Actors in a Kabuki play wear striking costumes and makeup. They use elaborate gestures to show strong emotions. Kabuki is performed on a thrust stage. A narrow, raised platform extends through the audience from the stage to the back of the theater. The actors use the platform for dancing and for important entrances and exits. A female dancer developed Kabuki. But after the 1650s only men acted in the plays.

Kabuki is related to a form of Japanese puppet theater called Bunraku. In Bunraku the performers move around large dolls to act out a drama. One of the performers chants the words of the story. Puppet theater also has a long tradition in many other countries, including Indonesia, Turkey, India, and China. In Europe puppet shows presented favorite characters in entertaining stories.

In Europe during the 1600s many theaters began to use the proscenium, or arch, stage. This is the type of stage seen in many modern theaters.

Several actors in Europe and North America in the 1700s and 1800s

Bunraku is a Japanese form of puppet theater. The people who move the puppets appear on the stage with the puppets.

developed new ideas about acting. Before then actors often read their parts as if they were making a speech. The English actor David Garrick developed a more natural acting style. He delivered his lines in the spirit of the character he was playing.

In the 1800s New York City became the theatrical center of the United States, as London was in England. In the 1900s people began performing theater in a greater variety of places. More cities and towns around the world built new theaters.

▶ More to explore
Ballet • Circus • Dance • Drama • Opera

A crowd watches a play being performed at an outdoor theater in Kabul, Afghanistan.

Thimphu

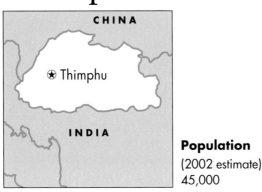

CHINA

⭑ Thimphu

INDIA

Population
(2002 estimate)
45,000

Thimphu is the capital of Bhutan, a
small country in south-central Asia. The
city lies on the Raidak River in a valley
of the Himalaya Mountains. It is a small
city. It does not have the crowds and
activity that many other capitals have.

Farming is the main economic activity
in Thimphu. Farmers grow rice, corn,
and wheat around the city. Thimphu has
few industries. The leading industries
process timber and make electricity from
waterpower.

Little is known about the early history of
Thimphu. The high mountains sur-

Farm crops grow close to an old Buddhist
religious building that now houses the government of Bhutan. In the distance is the city
of Thimphu.

rounding Bhutan long kept it separate
from the rest of the world.

For hundreds of years Bhutan had no set
capital. The center of government was
wherever the king lived. In 1962, however, Thimphu was named the capital.
The government then began making the
city more modern.

▶ **More to explore**
Bhutan

Thistle

Thistles are prickly plants that most
people think of as weeds. But some
kinds of thistle have nice flowers, and
people grow them as garden plants. One
type of thistle is the national symbol of
Scotland.

Thistles can grow to more than 8 feet
(2.4 meters) tall. They usually have
prickly leaves. The stem and flowers can
also be prickly. The leaves usually have
ragged edges. They are green or blue
green and are sometimes covered with
fine white hairs.

Thistles have many tiny flowers growing
together in tight clusters. The flowers are
packed so closely that the clusters look
like single flowers. Most types of thistle
can grow dozens of these flower clusters
on one plant. The flowers are mostly
pink, purple, or yellow. They produce
feathery seeds that scatter in the wind.

Thistles grow mostly from seeds. Some
thistles also can grow from small pieces
of root in the soil. This makes thistles

The "flowers" of a thistle are actually clusters of many tiny flowers.

hard to remove from farm fields. Thistles are also hard to get rid of because their roots grow deep into the soil. Also, livestock and other animals do not eat thistles because they are so prickly.

▶ **More to explore**
Plant • Scotland

Thorpe, Jim

Jim Thorpe was one of the greatest all-around athletes in history. He excelled at football, baseball, basketball, boxing, lacrosse, swimming, and hockey.

James Francis Thorpe was born on May 28, 1888, in Indian Territory, which is now Oklahoma. He was mostly of Native American descent. Thorpe attended Carlisle Indian Industrial School in Pennsylvania. There he played

football under the famous coach named Pop Warner.

In 1912 Thorpe went to the Olympic Games in Stockholm, Sweden. He won gold medals in the decathlon and the pentathlon. (The decathlon is a track-and-field competition with 10 events. The pentathlon has five events.) But in 1913 Thorpe's medals were taken away from him. It was found that Thorpe had played professional baseball in 1909 and 1910. A rule stated that professional athletes could not participate in the Olympics.

Thorpe played major league baseball from 1913 through 1919. Then, from

Jim Thorpe was a star player in the early days of American professional football.

1919 through 1926, he was an early star of American professional football. In 1920–21 he served as the first president of the organization that is now called the National Football League.

Thorpe died in Lomita, California, on March 28, 1953. The International Olympic Committee returned Thorpe's Olympic gold medals to his family in 1983.

Tibet

Tibet is a part of western China. It has some of the world's tallest mountains. Tibet is so high that it is often called the Roof of the World. The capital is Lhasa.

Most of Tibet is on a piece of land called the Plateau of Tibet. The plateau is a raised flat area about 15,000 feet (4,600 meters) above sea level. The Himalaya Mountains are to the south. Mount Everest, the world's highest peak, is on the border of Tibet and the country of Nepal. Tibet's climate is cold and dry.

Almost all the people of Tibet are Tibetans. Some Chinese also live there. Tibetans speak the Tibetan language and practice their own form of Buddhism. The main leader of Tibetan Buddhism is called the Dalai Lama.

The economy of Tibet is based on farming. Tibetans raise yaks, horses, cows, sheep, and goats. They grow barley, wheat, millet, buckwheat, and potatoes. Tibetans also make handicrafts such as carpets, blankets, jewelry, and wooden bowls. A few factories produce textiles, machinery, chemicals, and other goods.

Tibet became a powerful Buddhist kingdom between the AD 600s and 800s. It came under the rule of the Mongols in the 1200s. In the 1700s the Qing, or Manchu, Dynasty of China took over Tibet.

The Qing Dynasty lost power in 1912. Then the Dalai Lama ruled Tibet. But in 1950 China again took control. The Tibetans rebelled against the Chinese in 1959, but they were defeated. The Dalai Lama fled to India. In the 1960s and 1970s the Chinese closed Buddhist monasteries and temples and destroyed

The Potala Palace in Tibet was once the home of the Dalai Lama.

religious writings. In the 1980s China began to allow some freedom in Tibet.

▶ **More to explore**
Buddhism • China • Dalai Lama • Himalayas

Tick and Mite

Ticks and mites are tiny animals that are found all over the world. They are related to spiders. Many ticks and mites are parasites. This means that they live on or inside other animals, which are called hosts.

Ticks can be more than an inch (2.5 centimeters) long, but most are much smaller. They can be hard-bodied or soft. Most hard ticks live in fields or woods. Soft ticks generally live in the host's home or nest.

Mites live in water and soil, on plants, and as parasites on animals. Some are so small that people can see them only with a microscope. Others can be 0.25 inch (6 millimeters) long.

Ticks and mites develop in stages from an egg into an adult. Hard ticks start and end each stage on the ground. At the end of each stage they attach to a host, such as a rodent, dog, or person. They suck the host's blood for a few days and then drop to the ground. They can go months without a meal as they wait for a host.

Ticks and mites can be very harmful. They can spread diseases to people, animals, and plants. For example, the deer

An American dog tick perches on grass while it waits for a chance to attach itself to a dog or other mammal. The American dog tick can give humans a serious disease called Rocky Mountain spotted fever.

tick carries Lyme disease. Hard ticks can also give off nerve poisons that can paralyze or kill the host. Some mites cause itching and skin problems.

▶ **More to explore**
Lyme Disease • Parasite • Spider

Tide

Along the coasts of every ocean on Earth the water level changes on a regular basis. This movement is known as the tide. The greatest height reached as the water rises is known as high tide. The lowest level reached as the water falls is known as low tide.

Tides take place in all bodies of water. In some waters, however, the change is so slight that tides go unnoticed. Tides are easier to see where an ocean meets land along seacoasts and in bays. There are usually two high and two low tides per day at any given place. The times at which they happen, however, change from day to day. The average amount of time between two high tides is 12 hours and 25 minutes.

Tides are caused by a natural force called gravity. Because of gravity, all

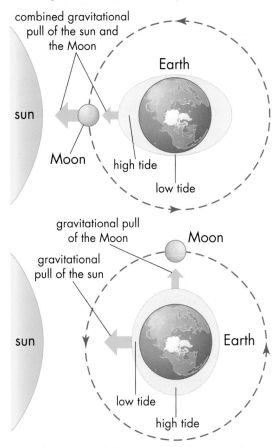

combined gravitational pull of the sun and the Moon

Earth

sun

Moon

high tide

low tide

gravitational pull of the Moon

Moon

gravitational pull of the sun

sun

Earth

low tide

high tide

Both the sun and the Moon pull on Earth's ocean water with a natural force called gravity. This pull creates tides. As the sun, Moon, and Earth move in space, they sometimes form a straight line, shown at top. This arrangement creates high tides that are higher than usual. It also creates low tides that are lower than usual. At other times the sun, Earth, and Moon are positioned like the corner of a square, shown at bottom. This arrangement evens out the tides more. It creates high tides that are less high than usual and low tides that are less low than usual.

bodies in the universe pull on each other. The sun and the Moon both pull on Earth, but the Moon has a greater influence because it is closer to Earth than the sun. As the Moon pulls on Earth it makes the water move. On the side of Earth near the Moon, the water builds up in a wave. Another wave forms on the other side of Earth. This is because the Moon is pulling Earth away from the water on that side. These waves result in high tide. As Earth rotates and the Moon moves around Earth, the tides change as well. Because the Moon moves around Earth in a regular path, the cycle of the tides follows a regular pattern.

▶ **More to explore**
Earth • Gravity • Moon • Sun

Tierra del Fuego

Tierra del Fuego is a group of islands at the southern tip of South America. About two thirds of the islands are in Chile, and the rest are in Argentina.

The name Tierra del Fuego is Spanish for "land of fire." The explorer Ferdinand Magellan named the islands. When he sailed around the tip of South America in the 1500s, he saw many fires built by Indians along the coast.

A waterway called the Strait of Magellan separates the islands from mainland South America. The main island, called Tierra del Fuego, is triangular. The southern and western parts of the islands are mountainous.

© 2006 Encyclopædia Britannica, Inc.

Forests of beech trees grow in the middle of the main island.

Chile's only oil field is in the northern part of Tierra del Fuego. The islands have some textile and electronics companies. There is some logging in the forests. Tourism is a valuable industry, too.

The first people to live on the islands were the Ona, Yahgan, and Alacaluf Indians. Magellan sailed past the islands in 1520. Gold was discovered on Tierra del Fuego in the 1880s. Then people from Argentina and Chile started moving to the islands. Oil was found in the area in 1945.

▶ **More to explore**
Argentina • Chile • Magellan, Ferdinand

Tiger

The tiger is the largest of the cats. Like lions, tigers are very strong and fierce hunters. Tigers are found in the wild only in parts of Russia, China, and South and Southeast Asia. They live in forests, grasslands, and swamps. The scientific name of the tiger is *Panthera tigris*.

Physical Features

Male tigers can grow to more than 3 feet (1 meter) high and 10 feet (3 meters) long, including the tail. They usually weigh between 350 and 640 pounds (160 to 290 kilograms). Their fur can range from light yellow on the belly to deep yellow or orange on the back. Dark stripes cover the head, body, and legs. There are also black rings on the tail.

There are five different kinds of tiger. The best known is the Bengal tiger, found mainly in India. The rare Siberian tiger is larger and has longer, softer fur. The Bengal and Siberian tigers are the kinds most often seen in zoos.

Behavior

Tigers hunt alone at night. They prey on animals such as deer and wild hogs. Tigers generally avoid large animals such as elephants and bears. They also try to stay away from people. But sometimes they attack people to save themselves or because they cannot find other food.

A tiger crouches in the grass and watches its prey before attacking it. It grabs the prey with its paws and bites the animal's neck. Then the tiger drags the dead animal to a safe place and eats it over several days.

Siberian tiger

Life Cycle

Tigers normally come together only to mate. About three months after mating, the female has two or three cubs. She looks after them for about two years and teaches them to hunt. Tigers live about 11 years.

Tigers and Humans

Tigers are endangered, or in danger of dying out. People have moved onto land where tigers once lived, destroying their homes. Plus, people hunt tigers for sport and for their skin. Many countries now have laws to protect tigers.

▶ **More to explore**
Cat • Lion

Tigris River

The Tigris River of southwest Asia is 1,180 miles (1,900 kilometers) long. It begins in the mountains of eastern Turkey. It then touches the northeastern border of Syria and crosses Iraq. In southeastern Iraq the Tigris joins the Euphrates River. The two rivers together

© 2006 Encyclopædia Britannica, Inc.

form the Shatt Al-'Arab. That waterway empties into the Persian Gulf.

The land that the Tigris flows through gets little rainfall. It is also very hot. But farmers are still able to grow crops there. They water their crops using water from the Tigris and the Euphrates. The watering methods they use are called irrigation.

Some of the earliest known civilizations began on the land between the Tigris and the Euphrates. The ancient Greeks called the area Mesopotamia. The name means "land between the rivers." Several ancient cities were built along the Tigris. One was Assur. That city gave its name to the empire called Assyria. Nineveh was another ancient city on the river. It was Assyria's capital. The main modern cities on the Tigris are Baghdad and Mosul, both in Iraq.

▶ **More to explore**
Euphrates River • Irrigation
• Mesopotamia

Tile

▶ *see* Brick and Tile.

Time

People use the idea of time to measure how long it takes for things to happen. They also use time to describe how long ago things happened in the past. Time helps to describe when things may happen in the future as well.

Units of Time

People divide time into days and hours. There are 24 hours in one full day and night. Hours are divided into minutes and seconds. There are 60 minutes in an hour and 60 seconds in a minute.

People measure longer periods of time by years. There are 365 or 366 days in one year. A year is divided into 12 months. Months have from 28 to 31 days.

Time Zones

At any time, only part of Earth experiences daylight. It is nighttime for the rest of the planet. This means that it cannot be the same time of day in every part of the world. For this reason people have divided the globe into 24 sections called time zones. At most places inside a time zone, it is the same time of day.

Imaginary lines separate all the time zones. The lines run from the North Pole to the South Pole. The first time zone begins at 0° longitude, or the prime meridian. This imaginary line runs through Greenwich, England.

When people cross one of the imaginary lines, they enter a new time zone. The time of day changes by one hour. If they cross into a time zone to the west, it is one hour earlier. If they cross into a time zone to the east, it is one hour later. (In a few places in the world, the time changes by only a half hour.)

The imaginary lines dividing the time zones are not always straight. They often bend west or east. This allows whole countries or regions to be within a single

A stopwatch measures the minutes and seconds an athlete takes to complete a run. People use many different types of watches, clocks, and calendars to keep track of time.

time zone. However, large countries—such as the United States and Russia—are divided into several time zones.

On the other side of Earth from the prime meridian is the International Date Line (IDL). It runs through the Pacific Ocean at about 180° longitude. When travelers cross the IDL going from west to east, they gain a whole day on the calendar. For example, if they start traveling on January 2, the date changes to January 1 when they cross the IDL. When people travel from east to west across the IDL, they move a day forward in time.

History

Ancient people measured time by looking at the sky. They saw the sun rise and set and the Moon grow full. They watched the stars and the other planets change position. They also experienced the days becoming shorter and longer and the cycle of the seasons.

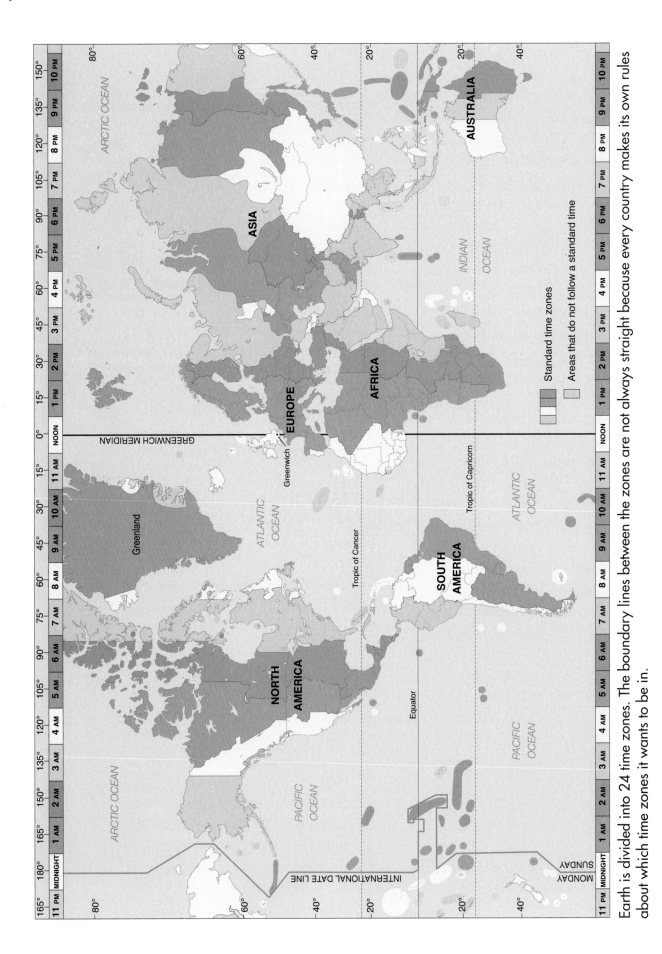

Earth is divided into 24 time zones. The boundary lines between the zones are not always straight because every country makes its own rules about which time zones it wants to be in.

People in ancient Egypt, Mesopotamia, Central America, and other places created calendars to keep track of the passing days. The ancient Egyptians also invented a form of clock called a sundial. Sundials cast shadows that move as the day passes.

Eventually people all over the world had developed many types of clocks and calendars to keep track of time. But the time was different in every city. In the 1800s some people thought there should be one system of measuring time so that everyone could agree about what time it is. This was important for such things as making schedules for trains and knowing when to go to school. In 1884 countries throughout the world adopted the time zone system that is still in use.

▶ More to explore
Calendar • Clock • Latitude and Longitude • Season • Sundial

Tiranë

Population
(2001 census)
343,078

Tiranë is the capital of Albania, a country in southeastern Europe. It lies on the Ishm River. It is Albania's largest city.

People crowd Tiranë's main square at night.

Tiranë is Albania's main center of business and industry. However, in the early 21st century the country's economy was one of the poorest in Europe. Factories in Tiranë make clothing, processed foods, leather, and other products.

A Turkish general founded Tiranë in the early 1600s. Albania was then part of the Turkish Ottoman Empire. Tiranë gradually grew into a busy trading center.

Albania became an independent country in 1912. Tiranë became its capital in 1920. Between 1939 and 1944, during World War II, Italian and then German forces controlled the city.

Between 1946 and the early 1990s, Albania was a Communist country. Protests in Tiranë helped to bring an end to Communist rule. However, the end of Communism did not bring about a lasting peace. In the later 1990s the city was the site of several violent political protests.

▶ More to explore
Albania

Titanic

The passenger ship called the *Titanic* sank in 1912, on its first voyage.

On its first trip across the Atlantic Ocean, a passenger ship called the *Titanic* struck a huge iceberg. The ship sank on April 15, 1912, killing more than 1,500 people. It was one of the most famous disasters of the 20th century.

Before there were airplanes, people crossed oceans on ships called ocean liners. The *Titanic* was one of the largest ocean liners of its time. It was more than 880 feet (270 meters) long and had nine decks, or floors. The hull, or body, was made of steel and divided into 16 compartments. Some people said that the *Titanic* was unsinkable.

On April 10, 1912, the *Titanic* set out from Southampton, England. It was bound for New York City. Some of the passengers were rich people on business or pleasure trips. Others were poor European emigrants who were looking for a better life in North America.

Lookouts saw an iceberg at 11:40 PM on April 14. The ship could not move out of the way fast enough. The hull was torn apart and the ship began to fill with water. At 2:20 AM the next day, the *Titanic* sank.

About 705 people escaped in lifeboats. However, there were not nearly enough lifeboats for the 2,224 people that the ship carried. Governments strengthened safety rules for ships after the disaster.

In 1985 deep-sea explorers found the remains of the *Titanic* at a depth of 13,000 feet (4,000 meters) near the Canadian island of Newfoundland. Underwater vessels explored the ship and brought pieces of wreckage to the surface.

▶ More to explore
Iceberg • Ship

Titans

In ancient Greek mythology the Titans were giants who once ruled the world. According to legend, they were the children of Uranus (Heaven) and Gaea (Earth). Uranus hated his children, and he shut them up in the Earth. The Titans rebelled against him and took power. Cronus (Saturn) then became the ruler of the Titans.

Later Cronus' son Zeus led a long war that forced the Titans from power. Zeus then became the chief god.

Other important Titans included Rhea, who was the wife of Cronus and the mother of Zeus. The Titan called Hyperion was the father of the sun, Moon, the Titan Prometheus helped human-kind by giving people fire.

▶ **More to explore**
Atlas • Greece, Ancient • Mythology • Prometheus • Zeus

Tlingit

The Tlingit are Native Americans of southern Alaska and northern British Columbia, in Canada. They live along the coast and on nearby islands in the Pacific Ocean.

The Tlingit traditionally got much of their food by fishing. They also hunted seals and sea otters and gathered wild berries and roots. The Tlingit used cedar wood from nearby forests to build houses. Their houses were large enough for several families.

In 1741 Russian explorers arrived in Tlingit lands. By the end of the 1700s Russian traders had set up a fort in Tlingit territory. Many Tlingit fell ill with deadly diseases carried by the Russians and other European settlers. In the 1830s smallpox killed about half of the Tlingit.

In 1867 Russia sold Alaska to the United States. Then U.S. settlers began taking over the tribe's land. More settlers arrived after gold was discovered in the area in 1880.

In 1912 the Tlingit helped to form a group called the Alaska Native Brotherhood. This group worked to take back the lands of southern Alaska's Indians.

The Titans were a group of giants in the myths of ancient Greece. Among the more important Titans were Atlas, Hyperion, Prometheus, Cronus, and Rhea.

and dawn. Atlas was a Titan who had to carry the heavens on his shoulders. And

Tlingit gather in Sitka, Alaska, in 2004 to remember a battle with Russian soldiers that took place in 1804.

In 1971 the U.S. government returned 44 million acres (18 million hectares) of land to the Tlingit and other tribes.

At the end of the 20th century more than 9,000 Tlingit lived in the United States. Another 1,000 Tlingit lived in Canada.

▶ **More to explore**
Native Americans

Toad

Toads are small animals often confused with frogs. Toads, however, have dry, rough skin and short legs. Frogs have moist, smooth skin and longer legs.

Toads can be found in all but the coldest parts of the world. They are amphibians, meaning that they live on both land and water. However, toads generally spend more of their time on land than they do in the water.

Toads have squat, plump bodies. They do not have tails. They range from about 1 to 10 inches (2.5 to 25 centimeters) long. Their skin is usually brownish olive, often with some darker spots. One group, called variegated toads, has large back feet and are bright yellow, red, or green with black spots.

Toads are typically covered with bumps that look like warts. When a toad feels threatened it releases poison from the bumps. The poison can sting an enemy's eyes and mouth. The poison of some toads is strong enough to kill their enemies.

Toads are active mainly at night. They spend the day underground or hidden under leaves or stones. In the winter most toads enter a state of inactivity called hibernation. Some toads are inactive during hot and dry weather as well.

Toads move by short hops or by walking. They catch prey with their long, sticky tongues. Toads generally eat insects and worms. Some large toads, however, eat frogs and small rodents.

The natterjack toad lives in northern Europe.

Some toads, such as the Oriental fire-bellied toad, can be quite colorful.

Toads lay their eggs underwater. After a few days the eggs hatch into small, fish-like creatures called tadpoles. Tadpoles have tails and gills. The gills are structures that help them breathe underwater. Tadpoles eventually lose their tails and develop lungs and legs. They can then leave the water to live on land.

▶ **More to explore**
Amphibian • Frog • Hibernation

Tobacco

Tobacco is a plant that is grown for its leaves. The dried leaves are usually made into cigarettes, cigars, or pipe tobacco. Users light these products and breathe in the smoke. Tobacco also may be chewed or taken in the form of a powder.

All these products deliver a habit-forming drug called nicotine to the user. This drug makes it hard to stop using tobacco. But using tobacco can cause serious health problems, including lung cancer, breathing disorders, and heart disease.

Native Americans were the first people to grow tobacco plants. They used tobacco in ceremonies and as medicine. In the late 1400s and early 1500s European explorers learned about tobacco from the Native Americans. The Europeans established large farms called plantations in the Americas to grow the crop. They also brought tobacco back to their home countries.

Today people in many parts of the world grow and use tobacco. However, some governments have tried to limit its use. For example, some places do not allow smoking in public buildings.

Tobacco plants produce large leaves. The leaves are dried after they are picked.

▶ **More to explore**
Drug

Tobago

▶ *see* Trinidad and Tobago.

Togo

The tiny country of Togo sits north of the equator in West Africa. Togo's capital is Lomé.

Togo is a long, narrow country. In the south it has a short coastline on the Atlantic Ocean. Togo borders Ghana, Burkina Faso, and Benin. The Togo Mountains cross central Togo. Plains cover the north. Togo has a hot climate with dry and rainy seasons.

Grasslands and scattered trees cover most of Togo. Tropical forests grow in the southwest. Togo's animals include elephants, lions, monkeys, hippopotamuses, crocodiles, lizards, and snakes.

Togo has many different ethnic groups. The two largest groups are the Ewe in the south and the Kabre in the north. Most of the people practice Christianity, African religions, or Islam. French is the national language. Most people live in small villages.

Women shop at an outdoor market in Togo.

Most of Togo's people are farmers. The main food crops include cassava, yams, and corn. Many people raise sheep, goats, and pigs. Farmers also produce coffee, cocoa, and cotton. Fishing is another source of food.

The Ewe and the Kabre peoples lived in the region before the 1300s. In 1884 Germans took over the region. During World War I France gained control of part of the area.

In 1960 French Togoland gained independence. In 1967 a military general took power. He remained president until he died in 2005. Togo then elected his son as president.

▶ **More to explore**
Lomé

Facts About TOGO

Atlantic Ocean

Population
(2008 estimate)
6,762,000

Area
21,925 sq mi
(56,785 sq km)

Capital
Lomé

Form of government
Republic

Major cities
Lomé, Sokodé, Kpalimé, Atakpamé, Kara

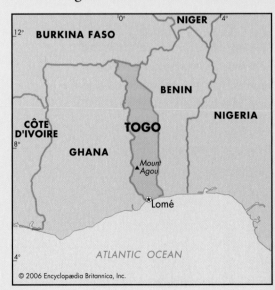

BURKINA FASO
NIGER
12°
0°
4°
BENIN
NIGERIA
CÔTE D'IVOIRE
TOGO
8°
GHANA
Mount Agou
Lomé
4°
ATLANTIC OCEAN
© 2006 Encyclopædia Britannica, Inc.

Tohono O'odham

The Tohono O'odham are Native Americans who live in southern Arizona and northern Mexico. They are often called the Papago. The Tohono O'odham are related to the Pima people. They may be descendants of the ancient Hohokam Indians.

The Tohono O'odham traditionally built houses from mud and brush in the desert. Their name means "desert people." Because their land was very dry, they moved in different seasons to make sure they had enough water. Summer rains provided water to grow crops. The tribe grew corn, beans, squash, and cotton. When the rains stopped, the

Tohono O'odham moved to winter villages in the mountains. There they got water from springs. For food, they hunted wild animals and gathered wild plants.

Spanish explorers arrived in the lands of the Tohono O'odham in the late 1600s. The Spanish taught the tribe how to grow wheat and raise cattle and horses.

The Tohono O'odham of Mexico eventually lost much of their land to settlers and ranchers. The Tohono O'odham of the United States were given several reservations. The Tohono O'odham Reservation in Arizona is the country's second largest reservation. In the late 20th century there were more than 17,000 Tohono O'odham in the United States. A few hundred lived in the Mexican state of Sonora.

▶ More to explore
Hohokam Culture • Native Americans • Pima

A photograph from the early 1900s shows a Tohono O'odham woman carrying a basket on her head.

Tokyo

Population (2008 estimate), city, 8,731,000; (2007 estimate), urban area, 35,700,000

Tokyo is the capital of Japan, an island country in eastern Asia. It is located on Japan's main island, Honshu. The city

Shibuya is a lively shopping district in Tokyo.

lies on Tokyo Bay, which is part of the Pacific Ocean. Tokyo is one of the largest cities in the world. It is Japan's center of industry, culture, and education.

The city of Tokyo is part of the huge Tokyo metropolitan area. It includes the countryside around Tokyo as well as several islands. The Tokyo metropolitan area also includes three other major cities—Yokohama, Kawasaki, and Chiba.

Cityscape

Tokyo has several distinct districts. At the heart of the city is the Imperial Palace, the home of the emperor of Japan. Many other national government buildings are in the nearby Kasumigaseki district. Marunouchi is a business district. Shinjuku is a center of entertainment and shopping. The Ginza district is world famous for its expensive stores.

Economy

Tokyo is Japan's main center of manufacturing, banking, and business man-

agement. Many companies have headquarters in the city. Publishing is a leading industry. Factories in Tokyo make such products as computers, televisions, and other electronics. Factories in the metropolitan area produce metals, chemicals, and machinery.

History

In ancient times the city was named Edo. It was a small village until the Tokugawa family began ruling Japan in the early 1600s. The Tokugawa rulers made Edo their headquarters. The city then grew greatly. In the 1800s more than a million people lived there. However, Japan's official capital was the city of Kyoto.

The emperor Meiji began ruling Japan in 1868. Edo was then renamed Tokyo and made the official capital. Under Meiji's rule the city was made more modern.

An earthquake severely damaged Tokyo in 1923 and killed at least 100,000 people. Bombing destroyed much of the city in the 1940s, during World War II. But Tokyo was soon rebuilt. In the second half of the 1900s it developed into an industrial center. It also became known for its many modern skyscrapers.

▶ **More to explore**
Japan

Tolkien, J.R.R.

J.R.R. Tolkien wrote popular books of fantasy fiction. The most famous of his

J.R.R. Tolkien

The Lord of the Rings, published in 1954 and 1955, also takes place in Middle-earth. This novel is sometimes divided into three parts: *The Fellowship of the Ring*, *The Two Towers*, and *The Return of the King*.

Tolkien died on September 2, 1973. He had started another book about Middle-earth, called *The Silmarillion*, but did not finish it. Tolkien's son Christopher published this book in 1977.

books are *The Hobbit* and *The Lord of the Rings*.

John Ronald Reuel Tolkien was born on January 3, 1892, in South Africa. At age 4 he moved with his family to Great Britain. Tolkien graduated from Oxford University in 1915. Soon afterward he left to fight for the British in World War I.

In 1925 Tolkien began teaching at Oxford. His classes dealt with the roots of the English language. He studied old fables, myths, and legends. During this time Tolkien began writing fantasy stories. Part of this writing included making up an entire language called Elvish. The characters called elves in Tolkien's stories speak this language.

Tolkien published *The Hobbit* in 1937. He wrote it partly to amuse his four children. The main character of the book is a short, furry-footed creature called a hobbit. The story takes place in a fantasy world called Middle-earth.

Toltec

The ancient Toltec people developed a great civilization in what is now central Mexico. From the AD 900s to the 1100s they were the most powerful Native Americans in the region.

The capital city of the Toltec was Tula. Historians do not know exactly where Tula was. However, they know that it

Stone columns that stand 15 feet (4.6 meters) high were carved by the Toltec in Mexico.

was in the area of what is now Mexico City. As many as 40,000 people lived in Tula.

The Toltec built houses out of clay bricks. These bricks kept the heat out in the summer and the cold out in winter. In Tula the Toltec also built great pyramids and palaces.

The Toltec farmed for most of their food. They grew corn and squash. They also grew cotton and plants that they used to make medicines.

The Toltec settled in what is now central Mexico in about AD 900. In the 1100s other Indian groups began invading Toltec lands from the north. The invaders were called the Chichimec. The Chichimec destroyed Tula in about 1160.

The Chichimec took on many Toltec ways of life. Among the Chichimec groups were the Aztec. They created the next great Indian civilization in central Mexico.

▶ **More to explore**
Aztec • Native Americans

Tomatoes come in different sizes and shapes. Some small varieties are called cherry tomatoes or grape tomatoes.

Tomato

Tomatoes are commonly called vegetables, but they are actually fruits. They are eaten raw or used in cooking. Canned tomatoes and tomato juice are also popular. Tomatoes are grown in all mild regions of the world. They belong to the nightshade family.

Tomato plants generally have many spreading branches. The leaves are hairy and have a strong smell. The flowers are yellow and hang in clusters. The fruit is about 0.5 to 3 inches (1.3 to 7.6 centimeters) across. It can be round or oval or shaped like a pear. When ripe, the fruit is soft, juicy, and usually red or yellow. Tomatoes contain many small seeds surrounded by jellylike pulp. This pulp contains most of the tomato's vitamin C.

Tomato plants first grew wild in the Andes Mountains of South America. The Spanish brought tomatoes to Europe after finding them growing in the Americas. At first Europeans grew tomatoes only for decoration. They thought that tomatoes were poisonous because they are related to the deadly nightshade plants. Tomatoes did not become popular in the United States until the early 1900s.

▶ **More to explore**
Fruit • Nightshade

Tonga

Schoolchildren in Tonga raise their hands to answer the teacher's question.

The country of Tonga is made up of about 170 islands in the southern Pacific Ocean. The largest island is Tongatapu. It is where the capital, Nuku'alofa, is located.

Tonga is a part of the Pacific region called Oceania. People live on only about 40 of Tonga's islands. Some islands are the peaks of underwater volcanoes. Others are atolls, or coral reefs that surround a pool of water. Tonga's climate is warm and rainy.

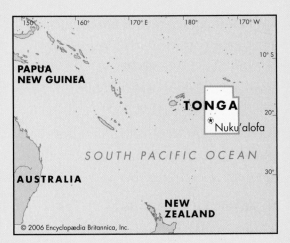

Rain forests grow on the volcanic islands. Mangrove trees grow in swampy areas. Tonga's birds include doves, kingfishers, cuckoos, and shrikes. Large fruit bats, called flying foxes, live on Tongatapu.

Almost all the people of Tonga are Polynesians, the native people of eastern Oceania. The main languages are Tongan and English. Nearly all Tongans are Christians. About two thirds of the people live on Tongatapu. Fewer than half of the people live in cities.

The economy of Tonga is based on farming and fishing. Farmers grow squash, coconuts, cassava, yams, bananas, and vanilla beans. They also raise pigs, goats, and cattle. Tourism is another important part of the economy.

People have lived on the islands for at least 3,000 years. Kings and queens have ruled Tonga since the AD 900s.

Dutch and British explorers visited the islands in the 1600s and 1700s. Christian missionaries arrived in the 1800s. In 1900 Tonga gave control of its foreign affairs to Great Britain.

Tonga became independent of Britain in 1970. In the 1990s some Tongans began asking the king to make the country a democracy.

▶ **More to explore**

Nuku'alofa • Oceania

Facts About TONGA

Population (2008 estimate) 103,000

Area 290 sq mi (750 sq km)

Capital Nuku'alofa

Form of government Constitutional monarchy

Major towns Nuku'alofa, Neiafu, Haveluloto

Tongue

The tongue is an organ, or body part, in the mouth. It is made up of a group of muscles. Most vertebrates, or animals with a backbone, have a tongue.

The tongue is firmly attached to the bottom of the mouth. This attachment keeps the tongue from being swallowed. The underside of a mammal's tongue is smooth. The top of the tongue is rough and bumpy. These bumps are called papillae. The papillae contain taste buds. They also produce some of the fluid in saliva, a sticky liquid that keeps the mouth moist.

The Human Tongue

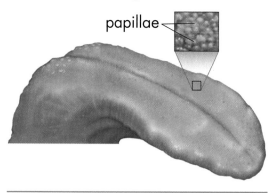

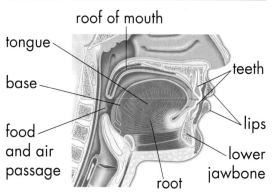

The drawing on the top shows papillae on the tongue. The drawing on the bottom shows how the tongue fits into the mouth.

Eating and Tasting

In many animals the tongue helps in chewing and swallowing food. Papillae help to grip and hold food. The front muscles of the tongue move food around and over the teeth during chewing. The back muscles of the tongue help in swallowing. They push chewed food to the back of the mouth and down the throat.

The tongue is also responsible for the sense of taste. The taste buds contain special cells that send information about foods to the brain. These special cells each respond to a particular kind of taste. Humans can sense five basic tastes: salty, sweet, sour (acid), bitter, and umami. Umami represents the taste of certain chemicals called amino acids.

People are born with about 10,000 taste buds, and there may be 50 to 150 cells in each bud. As people age, the number of taste buds may drop to 5,000. This may explain why some foods taste stronger to young people.

Other Uses

Tongues have many other uses. The human tongue plays an important part in speaking. It forms and shapes the sounds that make up language. Dogs and cats use their tongues to clean themselves. Frogs use their tongues to catch insects and other small animals for food. Snakes and other reptiles flick out their tongues to collect scents in the air.

▶ **More to explore**
Mouth • Muscle

Tonsillitis

Tonsillitis is an infection of the tonsils. The tonsils are oval-shaped lumps of tissue in the throat. Usually they help protect the body against disease. But sometimes they become infected themselves. An infection is an attack by tiny germs that cause disease. Children get tonsillitis more often than adults.

The germs that cause tonsillitis are called bacteria and viruses. Infected tonsils become large and red. A person with tonsillitis first feels a sore throat. The sore throat sometimes makes it painful to talk or to swallow. The person might also get a fever. Glands on the sides of the neck might swell.

Tonsillitis spreads easily, especially by coughs and sneezes. Avoiding people with tonsillitis reduces the chance of infection. Frequent hand washing also helps. Washing the hands can kill the bacteria and viruses that cause tonsillitis.

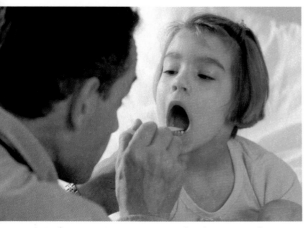

A doctor examines a girl's throat. When a child has a sore throat, the doctor often checks for tonsillitis.

The treatment of tonsillitis depends on the cause. If bacteria are the cause, the doctor gives the person a medicine called an antibiotic. If a virus is the cause, the tonsillitis usually has to clear up on its own. Tonsillitis generally lasts less than a week. During that time the person should rest and drink lots of liquids. In some severe cases of tonsillitis, a doctor has to remove the tonsils.

▶ **More to explore**
Bacteria • Virus

Topeka

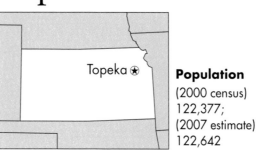

Population
(2000 census)
122,377;
(2007 estimate)
122,642

Topeka is the capital of the U.S. state of Kansas. The city lies on the Kansas River.

Many people in Topeka work for the government or in trade, health care, or other service industries. The city is an important market for wheat grown in the surrounding area. The leading manufacturing industries include printing, food processing, and making tires.

In its early history Topeka played a role in the U.S. conflict over slavery. A group of people who opposed slavery founded the city in 1854. Several battles took place there. Groups fought over whether

A sculpture honoring pioneers stands near the Kansas state Capitol in Topeka, Kansas.

Kansas should permit slavery when it became a U.S. state. In 1861 Kansas became a state that did not allow slavery. Topeka was made the capital.

In the 1860s Topeka became the headquarters for the building of a large railway. The railway brought jobs to the city and helped it grow.

In 1951 the Kansas River overflowed and flooded Topeka. A tornado damaged much of the city in 1966.

▶ **More to explore**
Kansas • Slavery

Torah

A holy text of Judaism, the Torah is made up of the first five books of the Hebrew Bible (which Christians call the Old Testament). These books are Genesis, Exodus, Leviticus, Numbers, and Deuteronomy.

The Torah begins with the story of the creation of the world. It goes on to explain and interpret the laws of God, including the Ten Commandments. Jews believe that God gave the laws of the five books to the prophet Moses on Mount Sinai.

All Jewish synagogues, or places of worship, keep a copy of the Torah. The copy is written by hand on parchment scrolls (rolled-up sheets of animal skin). During most synagogue services a member of the congregation reads from the Torah. Most synagogues read the entire Torah in one year.

In Hebrew the word Torah means "to teach" or "to show the way." In that broad sense, all Jewish teachings—including the Hebrew Bible, the Talmud, and unwritten Jewish traditions—can be considered part of the Torah.

▶ **More to explore**
Bible • Judaism • Moses • Talmud

The Torah is a Jewish holy text. Each copy is handwritten on rolled-up sheets of animal skin.

Toussaint-Louverture

Toussaint-Louverture

Toussaint-Louverture was born a slave but became a great military leader. He led the fight for the independence of Haiti. Haiti occupies part of the island of Hispaniola in the West Indies.

Early Life

François Dominique Toussaint was born in about 1743 in Saint-Domingue (now Haiti). He was black, like most of the other slaves in Saint-Domingue. Although he was a slave, he learned some French and Latin. As a young man he supervised the work of other slaves on the large farm where he lived. He became free in 1777.

Rebel Leader

During most of Toussaint's life, France controlled Saint-Domingue. But the slaves greatly outnumbered the French people living there. In 1791 the slaves rose up in rebellion. Toussaint formed his own rebel army. He soon became known as Toussaint-Louverture. This was because he easily found openings in the enemy's defenses. ("Louverture" comes from the French word for "opening.")

France fought to end the rebellion. But by 1801 Toussaint had taken over all of Hispaniola. He freed everyone on the island who was still a slave. He then made himself governor-general for life.

Capture and Death

Toussaint ruled until 1802. In that year France sent troops to take back control. Toussaint's forces were outnumbered. In 1803 the French captured Toussaint and sent him to France. He died in a French prison on April 7, 1803.

Another black leader named Jean-Jacques Dessalines continued the fight against France. His forces won independence for Saint-Domingue—renamed Haiti—in 1804.

▶ **More to explore**
Haiti • Slavery

Toy

Children everywhere enjoy playing with toys. A toy can be a simple ball, a game, or an expensive machine that uses the latest technology. Years ago most toys were made from wood and cloth. Today the most common material is plastic.

Toys date back to ancient times. Scientists often find toys when they dig up old ruins. These include ancient balls,

Did You Know?

Teddy bears have been popular toys for more than 100 years. They are named after Theodore "Teddy" Roosevelt, who was U.S. president from 1901 to 1909.

Simple wooden blocks decorated with numbers and letters are a popular toy.

dolls, tops, and toy wagons and boats. They have also dug up game pieces. People have played games similar to chess, checkers, and backgammon for thousands of years.

Many toys, from both ancient and modern times, look like objects from the adult world. As children grow they often imitate adults in their play. They enjoy toys modeled after things that adults use in everyday life. A child in ancient Egypt might have played with a small wooden camel. A child in today's world might have a toy car or a toy telephone.

The modern toy industry is a very big business. Simple toys are still common. But many companies produce toys that run on batteries. Other toys use the latest electronic and computer technology.

The toy business is challenging, however, because fads quickly come and go. A toy loved by children today may soon lose popularity. Safety is another concern for toy makers. Most toy packaging includes safety warnings. These messages warn about such things as small objects that a very young child could swallow.

▶ **More to explore**
Electronic Games

Track and Field

Contests of running, jumping, and throwing are called track-and-field events in the United States. In other countries this group of sporting events is called athletics. Track and field is the oldest form of organized sport. It is a major part of the Summer Olympic Games.

Track Meets and Events

Track-and-field events take place during a competition called a meet, or track meet. Track meets can be held either indoors or outdoors. Most meets take place in outdoor stadiums. These stadiums have a grass infield surrounded by an oval running track.

The contests in a meet are divided into track events and field events. In the track events athletes race against each other. The track used for outdoor running events measures 400 meters around. (One meter is equal to 3.3 feet.) The track is divided into running lanes. All the other events in a meet—the jumps and the throws—are field events. Field events are normally held in the grass infield.

Running Events

Short-distance races are called sprints. They cover distances of 100 meters, 200

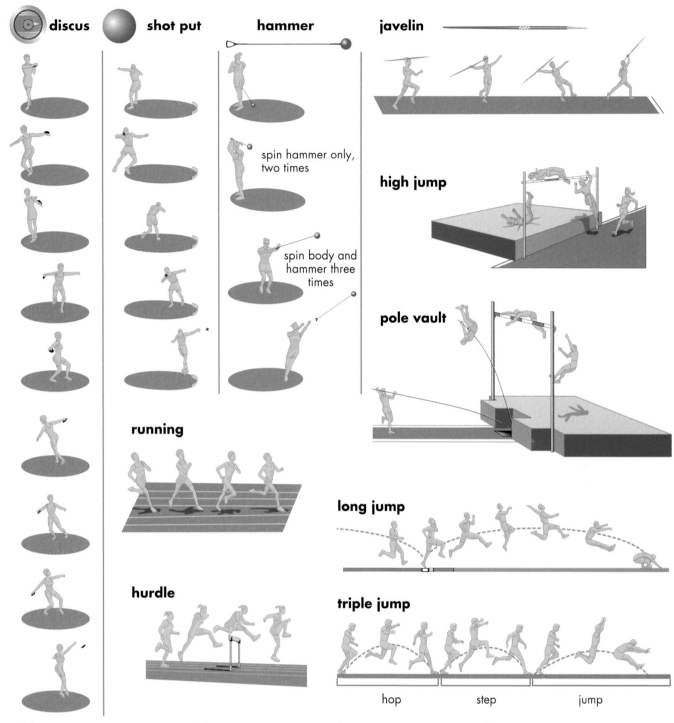

discus shot put hammer javelin

spin hammer only, two times

spin body and hammer three times

high jump

pole vault

running

long jump

hurdle

triple jump

hop   step   jump

Athletes compete in a variety of throwing, jumping, and running events at a track meet.

meters, and 400 meters. Sprinters need to get a quick start. Then they run at top speed for the whole race.

Middle-distance races cover 800 to 2,000 meters. Like sprinters, middle-distance runners need speed. But unlike sprinters, they do not always run at top speed. They need to adjust their speed to make sure that they have enough strength to run a longer distance. This strategy is called pacing.

Long-distance races cover 3,000 meters or more. Speed is not as important in long-distance races as it is in shorter races. Above all, long-distance runners need good physical conditioning. They have to be able to run for a long time. The marathon is a long-distance race that covers 26 miles 385 yards (42.2 kilometers). Marathons are run on roads. Cross-country races are long-distance events run on natural land.

There are several other types of running events. Relay races involve four runners per team. Each team member runs one fourth of the race's total distance. Hurdling combines sprinting with jumping over barriers called hurdles. The steeplechase is a long-distance race in which runners jump over hurdles and water barriers.

Jumping Events

There are four jumping events at a track meet: the high jump, the pole vault, the long jump, and the triple jump. The high jump and the pole vault are called vertical jumps. The athlete who jumps

Pole vaulters use a long, flexible pole to launch themselves over a high bar.

the highest is the winner. High jumpers try to leap over a thin bar balanced between two supports. Pole vaulters also try to jump over a bar, but the bar is set higher. They use a long, flexible pole to gain height. The pole bends to launch the vaulter over the bar.

The long jump and the triple jump are called horizontal jumps. The athlete who jumps the farthest wins these events. In both events the athlete begins with a high-speed run. At the end of the run a long jumper takes a single leap forward. A triple jumper must perform a series of three actions: a hop, a step, and a jump.

Throwing Events

A track meet includes four throwing events: the shot put, the hammer throw, the discus throw, and the javelin throw. In each event athletes try to throw an

In the type of race called hurdling, runners jump over a series of barriers called hurdles.

object as far as possible. The shot is a heavy metal ball. The hammer is a metal ball connected by a strong wire to a handle. The discus is a plate-shaped disk. The javelin is a spear. The athlete who throws the object the farthest wins.

Decathlon and Heptathlon

The decathlon and the heptathlon are competitions that combine several events. They test all-around athletes. In the Olympics men compete in the decathlon and women compete in the heptathlon. Points are awarded in each event and added up to determine the winner.

The decathlon and the heptathlon each take two days to complete. The decathlon consists of 10 events: the 100-, 400-, and 1,500-meter runs, the 110-meter hurdles, the discus and javelin throws, the shot put, the pole vault, the long jump, and the high jump. The heptathlon consists of seven events: the 200- and 800-meter runs, the 100-meter hurdles, the high jump, the long jump, the shot put, and the javelin throw.

History

People in different cultures have held footraces and other track-and-field contests for thousands of years. The first records of the Olympic Games, held in Greece, date from 776 BC. At those Olympics there was only one event, a footrace. Later Olympics in Greece included a five-event competition. It consisted of a footrace, the long jump, wrestling, and javelin and discus throws. The ancient Olympics ended in the AD 300s.

Track and field as practiced today developed in England. There the sport dates back to the 1100s. But track and field was not well organized as a sport until the 1800s. The sport started becoming popular in the United States in the 1860s.

The Olympic Games began again in 1896. The Olympics helped to spread interest in track and field throughout the world. An organization called the International Association of Athletics Federations (IAAF) now governs track-and-field competition in the Olympics. It also approves all world records in track-and-field events.

▶ **More to explore**
Marathon • Olympic Games

Trade

Trade is the buying and selling of goods and services. Goods are objects that people grow or make—for example, food, clothes, and computers. Services

Machines move large containers of goods off a ship and onto trucks at a port in Canada. Shipping goods between countries is an important part of international trade.

are things that people do—for example, banking, communications, and health care. People have traded since prehistoric times. Today most countries take part in international trade, or trade across country borders.

Reasons for Trade

Many children enjoy trading baseball cards. A trade only happens when each person has a card or cards that the other person wants.

Trade happens because people need or want goods that they do not have. People also trade for services when they do not have the time or the skills to do things. Trade between countries happens for similar reasons. For example, some countries have resources, such as oil, or skills, such as car manufacturing, that other countries will buy.

Both people and countries want trade to benefit them. Families want to earn more money than they spend on goods and services. Countries try to sell, or export, as much as they buy, or import, from other countries.

Trade Limits

In some economies, the government controls all trade. In others, the government allows companies to trade more freely. However, even governments that support free trade control trade in some way. They may keep companies from trading dangerous or illegal products. They may also pass laws to prevent companies from forming monopolies. A monopoly occurs when one company has so much control over a certain type of good or service that no other companies can compete, or make money selling that good or service.

Countries also limit trade between other countries and themselves to protect their economies. Countries may charge tariffs, or special taxes, on foreign goods. They may also set quotas, or limits on the amount of foreign goods they buy.

Free Trade

In the 1900s many countries worked to stop trade limits. Some formed trading blocs, or groups of countries that trade freely. Examples include the North American Free Trade Agreement (NAFTA), the European Union, and South America's Mercosur. In addition, about 150 countries joined the World Trade Organization (WTO). The WTO encourages free trade around the world.

The lifting of trade limits caused international trade to grow. However, some people questioned the idea of free trade.

If governments did not oversee trade, they warned, international companies could pay workers poorly and pollute the environment.

History

Trade developed along with civilization. Before 2000 BC people in the earliest civilizations of Mesopotamia, ancient Egypt, and the Indus Valley traded among themselves and with other peoples. As time passed, civilizations built trade routes. They used these paths to transport spices, salt, gold, and other goods over greater distances. Trade routes went over land and sea.

In the AD 1400s Europeans began exploring by sea to find new trade routes to Asia. Some explored the coast of Africa. Others crossed the Atlantic Ocean to North and South America. By the 1600s Portugal, Spain, England, France, and the Netherlands had set up colonies, or settlements, around the world.

In the 1700s the Industrial Revolution began. This was a period when people invented machines to make goods in factories. This improved manufacturing and transportation, and trade increased. An idea called laissez-faire capitalism soon became popular. "Laissez-faire" is a French phrase that means "to let do." It meant that governments should not interfere with trade or other economic activities. It allowed companies and their owners to do whatever they wanted. Many became rich as a result.

Workers soon started labor movements to protest their poor treatment by rich companies. In the early 1900s World War I and the Great Depression led to a decline in trade. Many governments began to support workers and to control trade more strictly. The idea of free trade did not become popular again until after World War II (1939–45).

▶ **More to explore**
Capitalism • Civilization • Colony • Economics • Tax • Transportation

Trail of Tears

In 1838 and 1839 the U.S. government took away the homeland of the Cherokee people. It forced the Cherokee to travel from the Southeast to what is now Oklahoma. Most of them had to walk all the way. This event is known as the Trail of Tears.

In the early 1800s the Cherokee got along better with the United States than most other Native American groups. Then, in 1835, gold was found on

A painting shows Cherokee taking a long forced journey called the Trail of Tears. Thousands of them died along the way.

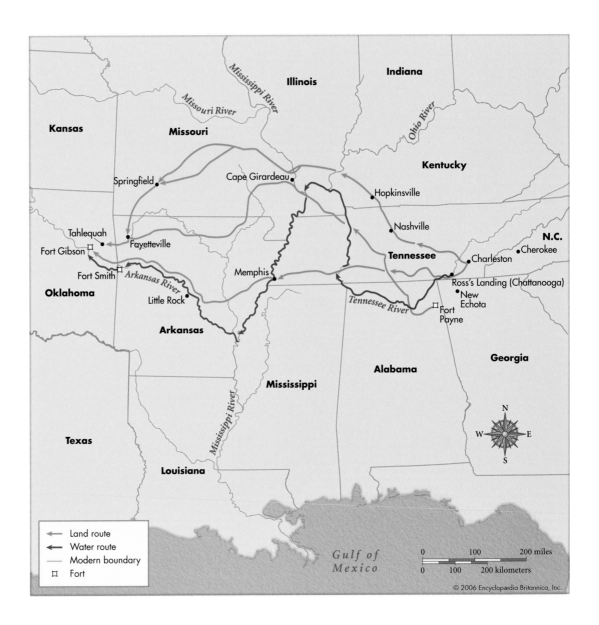

Cherokee land in Georgia. Some white people decided to take over the land and push the Cherokee out.

In 1835 a few Cherokee signed a treaty, or agreement, with the U.S. government. They agreed to sell all Cherokee land to the United States for 5 million dollars. But most of the tribe did not think the treaty was legal. The U.S. Supreme Court agreed with them.

President Andrew Jackson and Georgia officials ignored the Court's decision. In

the fall of 1838 U.S. troops began rounding up about 15,000 Cherokee and putting them in prison camps. Local residents burned their homes. Troops then sent the Cherokee west in groups of about 1,000.

The Cherokee suffered terribly on the march, which lasted 116 days. They had to walk in the cold, and they were not allowed to rest. They did not have enough food. Some went by boat in conditions that were just as bad. About 4,000 Cherokee died.

In Oklahoma the Cherokee were given some land. Many Cherokee still live there.

▶ **More to explore**
Cherokee • Jackson, Andrew • Native Americans

Transplant

During the type of surgery called a transplant, doctors remove a part from a person's body and then replace it with a similar part. A transplant is also called a graft. The purpose of a transplant is to replace a damaged or sick body part with a part that works.

The working part can be from the person's own body or from another person. The person who gets the body part is called the recipient. If another person gives a body part, that person is called the donor. Transplant donors can be living or dead.

When a doctor moves a body part from one place to another on the same person, the operation is called an autograft. One common type of autograft is a skin graft. This operation uses skin from one area of a person's body to replace lost skin on another area.

When a doctor transplants a body part from another person into a recipient, the operation is called an allograft. Allografts can be done with many body parts, including kidneys, livers, lungs, and intestines. These parts can come from living donors. Corneas (parts of eyes needed for sight) and hearts must

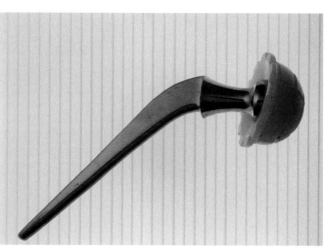

Doctors can replace a damaged hip joint with an artificial joint made out of metal and plastic.

come from dead donors. Doctors also can replace certain diseased parts, including heart valves and hip sockets, with artificial, or man-made, ones.

The main problem with transplants is rejection. When this happens the body's immune system treats the new part like a germ or an infection and tries to kill it. To prevent rejection doctors give recipients medicines that keep the body from attacking the new part.

▶ **More to explore**
Immune System • Surgery

Transportation

Transportation is a general word for all the methods people use to move themselves and their goods from one place to another. Just as they have for thousands of years, people today rely on walking to travel short distances. For longer distances, people depend on animals, bicycles, automobiles, trucks, railroads, ships, and airplanes.

Some people transport themselves through a city on foot. Others use trains or cars.

Reasons for Transportation

The world's economy depends on transportation. Raw materials must be moved from where they are produced to factories, where they are processed. Food, minerals, and wood often travel by truck, railroad, or ship. Oil and gas often travel by pipeline. Next, manufactured products must be moved from factories to stores. They may travel by truck, railroad, ship, or airplane.

People need transportation to get from home to work, too. Many people drive cars to work. Others take public transportation, including buses and trains. People also take cars, trains, ships, and airplanes to get to vacation spots and to visit family and friends. Some people drive just for enjoyment.

History

Early Transportation

Walking was the main method of transportation until humans domesticated, or tamed, animals. Camels, horses, and cattle then carried goods and people. More than 5,000 years ago people invented the wheel. This allowed animals to pull carts. Ancient peoples also traveled by water, at first with simple dugout canoes and rafts.

The Persians built a system of roads in the 500s BC. The ancient Egyptians, Indians, and Chinese also built roads. By the AD 200s the Romans had built roads across Europe.

Transportation by water expanded in the Middle Ages (AD 500–1500). New ships were built with multiple sails. They were able to travel farther and faster than earlier ships that were powered by rowing. Improvements in navigation made it possible to sail farther from land. Voyages of discovery in the 1400s and 1500s opened up trade routes between distant points.

Modern Transportation

The invention of the steam engine in the 1700s was an important event in transportation history. Steam-powered boats could easily travel upriver. Steam-powered ships could cross oceans without wind. On land, inventors used steam engines to power locomotives. This led to the growth of railroads. By 1869 a railroad ran across the United States, and steamships regularly crossed

An ocean liner unloads war prisoners during World War II (1939–45). Liners were an important means of transportation during the first half of the 1900s. In peacetime they carried rich people to vacation spots and poor immigrants to new homes.

the Atlantic Ocean. Trips that had taken weeks now took days.

Builders of canals made some ocean trips much shorter. The Suez Canal in Egypt shortened the trip between Europe and Asia by thousands of miles. The Panama Canal in Panama shortened the trip between the East and West coasts of North America.

The late 1800s saw the first successful bicycles and automobiles. They made quick and easy transportation available to more people than ever before. People who bought cars demanded more and better roads.

In 1903 the U.S. inventors Wilbur and Orville Wright flew the world's first airplane. The invention of the jet engine in the 1940s made air travel the fastest transportation in history.

Transportation Problems
Advances in transportation have led to problems, however. Cars and trucks cause traffic jams, accidents, and air pollution. These vehicles also use oil for fuel. The supply of oil is limited and controlled by a few countries. To ease crowded roads, governments have worked to improve public transportation. To fight pollution, scientists are developing vehicles that run on different types of fuel.

▶ **More to explore**
Airplane • Automobile • Bicycle • Boat • Canal • Navigation • Railroad • Road • Ship

Tree

Trees are tall, woody plants. They usually have a stem called a trunk. Trees are the largest and oldest living things on Earth. Some trees live for hundreds or even thousands of years. There are more than 80,000 species, or types, of tree. Well-known trees include birches, firs, maples, palms, and pines.

Groups of Trees
Scientists divide trees into groups based on how they reproduce. Some trees reproduce with spores, or particles that grow into new plants. They are called tree ferns. Most trees reproduce with seeds.

People grow eucalyptus trees for their wood and oil. The leaves of some kinds of eucalyptus contain an oil used in medicines.

Some seed-bearing trees grow their seeds in cones. They are called conifers. Most conifers have needle-shaped leaves. Other seed-bearing trees grow their seeds in fruits or pods. They are known as broad-leaved or flowering trees. They have broad, flat leaves.

Scientists also group trees based on whether they lose their leaves. Trees that keep their leaves year-round are called evergreens. Trees that lose their leaves at some point during the year are called deciduous trees.

Physical Features

Trees are usually more than 10 feet (3 meters) tall. They have roots, a trunk, branches, and leaves. The trunk and branches are made of fibers called wood. These fibers are protected by an outer covering called bark. As the tree ages, the trunk and branches thicken.

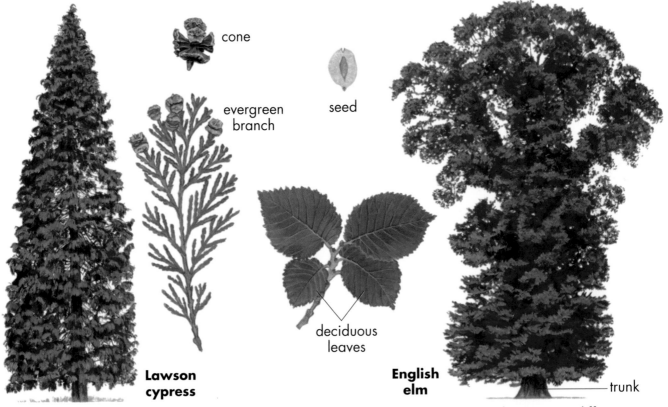

cone

evergreen branch

seed

deciduous leaves

Lawson cypress

English elm

trunk

The Lawson cypress and the English elm look different because they are two different types of tree. The Lawson cypress is a conifer and an evergreen. It produces seeds in cones and has needlelike leaves that stay on all year. The English elm is broad-leaved and deciduous. It produces seeds in fruits and has leaves that fall off in autumn.

The leaves make food for the tree through a process called photosynthesis. Veins run through the leaves. They carry water and food to and from the branches. Leaves are usually green. The leaves of deciduous trees often change colors in autumn before they fall off. New leaves then grow in spring.

Uses

Trees are very important to people. Tree wood is used to build homes and furniture. Paper is made from wood fibers. Many people burn wood to cook and to heat their homes. Farmers plant trees that grow fruit for people to eat.

Trees also help keep the air clean. They release oxygen for animals, including humans, to breathe. They take in the carbon dioxide that animals breathe out.

▶ More to explore

Bark • Birch • Conifer • Fir • Maple • Palm • Photosynthesis • Pine • Plant

Trenton

Population
(2000 census) 85,403; (2007 estimate) 82,804

Trenton is the capital of the U.S. state of New Jersey. In 1776, during the Ameri-

The State House in Trenton is the meeting place of the New Jersey General Assembly, or state legislature.

can Revolution, American troops won an important battle in the city.

Government is the largest employer in Trenton by far. Many other people in the city work in health care, trade, and other service industries. Factories in Trenton make medicines, metal products, and pottery.

The first Europeans to settle in the area that is now Trenton arrived in 1679. In 1714 a businessman named William Trent established the town. It was later named Trenton in his honor.

The battle of Trenton took place in December 1776, during the American

Revolution. General George Washington led American troops across the Delaware River. The next day they launched a surprise attack on British troops in Trenton. The Americans won the battle.

Trenton was the temporary capital of the United States in 1784 and again in 1799. It became the capital of New Jersey in 1790.

▶ **More to explore**
American Revolution • New Jersey

Triceratops

The dinosaur known as *Triceratops* looked something like a modern rhinoceros. However, it had three sharp horns on its head. The name *Triceratops* means "three-horned face." *Triceratops* also had a bony neck frill that surrounded the head like a huge collar.

When and Where *Triceratops* Lived

Triceratops lived about 70 to 65 million years ago. It was among the last dinosaurs to live on Earth before the dinosaurs disappeared. Fossils, or remains, of *Triceratops* have been found in North America.

Physical Features

Triceratops was the largest of the horned dinosaurs. It weighed up to 5 tons and reached a length of nearly 30 feet (9 meters). The skull and neck frill of *Triceratops* often measured more than 6 feet (2 meters) long. Each of the two horns above the eyes was longer than 3 feet (1 meter). The horn on the snout was short and thick. The massive body of *Triceratops* was supported by four sturdy legs. Its back legs were longer than its front legs. It had feet like an elephant. *Triceratops* had a fairly short, thick tail.

Behavior

Triceratops was a slow-moving plant eater. The neck frill acted as a protective shield against such enemies as *Tyrannosaurus rex*. *Triceratops* also used its long horns to defend itself and to fight rival males. *Triceratops* lived and traveled together in groups. Adults may have protected their young by forming an outward-facing circle around them.

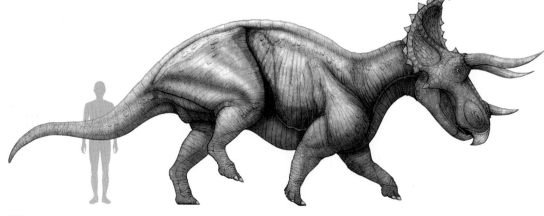

Triceratops

Trinidad and Tobago

Children dress in colorful costumes for a carnival celebration in Trinidad and Tobago.

The Republic of Trinidad and Tobago is an island country in the Caribbean Sea. The capital is Port of Spain.

The island of Trinidad is larger than the island of Tobago. Trinidad is only about 7 miles (11 kilometers) from the coast of Venezuela in South America. Both islands are mountainous. Trinidad has many short rivers, but Tobago has only a few streams. The country has a warm climate with dry and rainy seasons.

© 2006 Encyclopædia Britannica, Inc.

Tropical rain forests grow in the high areas. The islands' animals include golden tree frogs, porcupines, armadillos, wild pigs, and rodents. The scarlet ibis is the country's national bird.

Blacks and East Indians each make up about 40 percent of the population. Most of the rest of the people have mixed roots. English is the main language. More than half of the people are Christians. Many of the East Indians follow Hinduism or Islam.

Trinidad and Tobago has a strong economy. The country produces petroleum (oil) and natural gas. Manufacturing and tourism are also important to the islands. The country's products include sugar, chemicals, fertilizers, steel, and cement. Farmers grow sugarcane, oranges, rice, coffee, and cocoa.

Arawak Indians lived on Trinidad when Christopher Columbus arrived in 1498. As the Spanish took control, almost all the Indians died. French settlers came in the 1700s. They brought Africans with them as slaves. Great Britain took over Trinidad in 1797 and Tobago in 1814. The British brought people from India to work on plantations.

Trinidad and Tobago gained independence in 1962. The country discovered its huge oil and gas deposits in 1998.

▶ **More to explore**
Caribbean Sea • Port of Spain

**Facts About
TRINIDAD AND
TOBAGO**

Population
(2008 estimate)
1,305,000

Area
1,980 sq mi
(5,128 sq km)

Capital
Port of Spain

**Form of
government**
Republic

Major cities
Chaguanas, San
Fernando, Port of
Spain, Arima,
Point Fortin

Tripoli

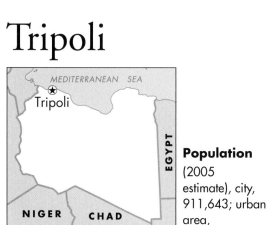

Population
(2005 estimate), city, 911,643; urban area, 2,098,000

Tripoli is the capital of Libya, a country in northern Africa. The city lies on a piece of rocky land overlooking the Mediterranean Sea. It is Libya's largest city and main seaport.

Shipping oil and other goods through the port brings money to Tripoli. The city is also Libya's main center of business and industry.

In ancient times the city was called Oea. People called the Phoenicians founded it in the 600s BC. It was one of the three main cities in the Phoenician region called Tripolitania, which means "Three

A child plays near the People's Palace in Tripoli, Libya. The building was the king's palace when Libya was a kingdom.

Cities." The city became part of the Roman Empire and later the Byzantine Empire.

Muslim Arabs conquered Tripoli and the rest of Libya in about AD 645. The Turkish Ottoman Empire ruled Libya from 1551 until 1911. Then Italy and, later, Great Britain controlled Libya. In 1951 Libya became an independent country with Tripoli as its capital.

▶ **More to explore**
Libya

Tropical Rain Forest

▶ *see* Rain Forest.

Tropics

The region of Earth's surface that is closest to the equator is called the tropics. Two imaginary lines that circle the globe mark the boundaries of the tropics. The line called the Tropic of Cancer marks the northern edge. Its latitude (distance from the equator) is 23° 27' N. The line called the Tropic of Capricorn marks the southern edge. Its latitude is 23° 27' S.

The tropics are the only part of Earth where the sun sometimes shines straight down. Because the sunlight is so strong, the tropics are generally warmer than other parts of Earth. Tropical temperatures are warm or hot throughout the year. The temperatures do not change

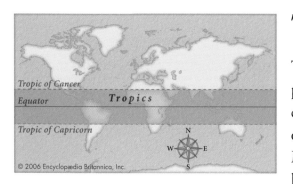

© 2006 Encyclopædia Britannica, Inc.

Trout

Trout are a kind of fish that many people like to catch and eat. Trout are closely related to salmon. Most species, or types, of trout are freshwater fish. Many live in clear, cool streams and lakes. Some types live in the ocean but return to freshwater to breed.

There are two main groups of trout species: black-spotted trout and speckled trout. The species of black-spotted trout include rainbow, cutthroat, and golden trout. Black-spotted trout range in color from silver, brown, or dark gray to shiny green, blue, red, or gold. They all have small black spots on the back.

The species of speckled trout include brook, Dolly Varden, lake, and bull trout. Some speckled species are also called chars. Speckled trout have lighter spots on a darker body. Many speckled species have pinkish or red spots, especially on the underside.

The brown trout is separate from the black-spotted trout and speckled trout. It has a brown body with black spots.

greatly, but winds and rain bring different types of weather. Most tropical places experience wet and dry seasons.

Areas closest to the equator are the wettest. A great deal of rain falls year-round. Dense rain forests cover the land. The largest tropical rain forests on Earth lie in Brazil and in parts of Africa.

The climate is drier in tropical regions that lie farther north and south of the equator. In these regions there are one or two dry seasons each year. The forests may be deciduous, meaning that the trees shed their leaves during the dry periods. Savannas, or grasslands with scattered trees, are also common.

The driest parts of the tropics lie near the northern and southern edges. Here the dry season is long. Few trees grow. Shrubs and low grasses cover the land. Two of Earth's big deserts, the Sahara and the Kalahari, lie on the edges of the tropics.

Many plants and other products that people value come from the tropics. Some of these are bananas, coffee, cocoa, tea, rubber, spices, nuts, and tropical wood.

▶ **More to explore**
Desert • Equator • Rain Forest

The rainbow trout is popular with people who fish for sport.

Trout vary in size, depending on the species. Many species of trout are about 1 foot (30 centimeters) long.

Trout eat insects, small fish, and eggs of other fish. Many species spawn, or reproduce, in the spring or the fall. The females bury their eggs in gravel nests that they dig in the bottom of streams. The eggs hatch after two or three months.

▶ **More to explore**
Fish • Salmon

Truman, Harry S.

After President Franklin D. Roosevelt died in 1945, Vice President Harry S. Truman became the 33rd president of

Harry S. Truman was the 33rd president of the United States.

the United States. Truman led the country through the end of World War II. After the war he worked to stop the spread of Communism.

Early Life and Career

Truman was born in Lamar, Missouri, on May 8, 1884. He was the oldest of the three children of John Anderson Truman, a farmer, and Martha Young. Harry graduated from high school in Independence, Missouri.

A member of the Missouri National Guard, Truman volunteered to serve in World War I in 1917. He fought in France and then returned to the United States in 1919. That year he married Elizabeth (Bess) Wallace. They had one daughter.

With an Army friend, Truman opened a men's clothing store in Kansas City. The business failed in the early 1920s.

Political Career

The Democrats who controlled Kansas City got Truman elected as a county judge in 1922. In 1934 he won a seat in the U.S. Senate.

In 1944 President Roosevelt chose Truman as his vice presidential running mate. After winning the election, Roosevelt died suddenly on April 12, 1945. Truman then became president.

Presidency

World War II in Europe soon ended, but war with Japan continued. Hoping to prevent more U.S. deaths by making

TIMELINE

May 8, 1884	1944	April 12, 1945	August 1945	1950	1953	December 26, 1972
Truman is born in Lamar, Missouri.		Roosevelt dies; Truman becomes president.		The Korean War begins.		Truman dies in Kansas City, Missouri.
	Truman is elected vice president under Franklin D. Roosevelt.		Truman orders atomic bombs dropped on Japan; World War II ends.		Truman retires from office.	

Japan surrender, Truman decided to use the newly invented atomic bomb in Japan. In early August 1945 U.S. airplanes dropped atomic bombs on the cities of Hiroshima and Nagasaki. The bombs killed more than 100,000 men, women, and children. Japan surrendered on August 14, 1945.

After the war Truman helped the United States join the United Nations, a new international peace organization. He also introduced the Truman Doctrine. That policy said that the United States would fight the spread of Communism, the political system of the Soviet Union.

In 1948 Truman approved the Marshall Plan. Under the plan the United States sent billions of dollars to help rebuild Europe. By strengthening the economies of western Europe, the plan prevented Communism from spreading there. That year Truman also ordered desegre-gation (the mixing of races) in the U.S. military.

After beginning his second term in 1949, Truman presented a program of reforms called the Fair Deal. He wanted more public housing, more money for education, higher wages, government-protected civil rights, and national health insurance. Congress did not pass most of the Fair Deal reforms, but citizens debated Truman's ideas for years to come.

The Korean War began during Truman's second term. In 1950 Communist North Korea invaded South Korea. Backed by the United Nations, Truman ordered U.S. military forces to help South Korea. The war dragged on past the end of Truman's presidency.

Retirement and Death

After his term ended in 1953, Truman retired to Independence, Missouri. He died in Kansas City, Missouri, on December 26, 1972.

▶ **More to explore**
Communism • Korean War • Roosevelt, Franklin D. • United Nations • United States • World War II

Truth, Sojourner

Sojourner Truth spoke out against slavery and for women's rights in the 1800s. Her courage and powerful way of speaking helped the causes of both African Americans and women in the United States.

Early Life
Truth was born a slave in the U.S. state of New York in about 1797. She was originally named Isabella Baumfree. Isabella worked for several different owners. Her last owner, Isaac Van Wagener, freed her just before slavery ended

Sojourner Truth

in New York in 1827. Isabella took the last name Van Wagener.

Speaking Out
In 1829 Isabella moved to New York City and worked as a house cleaner. In 1843 she left New York to become a traveling preacher. She also changed her name to Sojourner Truth.

Truth discovered that some people had started working to end slavery. This movement was called abolitionism. She began speaking out against slavery in the late 1840s. She soon became a popular abolitionist speaker throughout the North and the Midwest. In 1850 Truth published her life story, called *The Narrative of Sojourner Truth*.

Truth also defended women's rights. She complained that women could not vote or serve on juries. She also pointed out that they received less money than men for the same work.

Later Years
After the American Civil War started in 1861, Truth became even more famous. In 1864 she visited Washington, D.C., where she met President Abraham Lincoln. Also in 1864 Truth took a job with the National Freedmen's Relief Association, a group that helped former slaves.

In 1875 Truth retired to her home in Battle Creek, Michigan. She died there on November 26, 1883.

▶ **More to explore**
Abolitionist Movement • African Americans • Women's Rights

Tsar

Ivan IV, known as Ivan the Terrible, was the first Russian ruler to use the title of tsar.

When Russia had a royal family, the emperor was called the tsar. A Russian empress's title was tsarina, a prince's title was tsarevich, and a princess's title was tsarevna. Tsars ruled Russia from 1547 to 1917.

The term tsar (also spelled czar) is the Russian version of Caesar, the family name of Julius Caesar and the first emperors of Rome. The link between Rome and Russia was the Byzantine Empire, which began as the eastern branch of the Roman Empire and fell in 1453. In 1472 Ivan III, the prince of Moscow, married the niece of the last Byzantine emperor. Ivan III's grandson, Ivan IV, was the first Russian ruler to use the title of tsar. Known as Ivan the Terrible, he had great power and ruled harshly. Later tsars had similar qualities.

In 1721 Peter the Great stopped using the title of tsar. Even so, Russia's emperors continued to be called tsars until the last of them, Nicholas II, was removed from the throne. Revolutionaries killed Nicholas and his entire family in 1918 so that no descendants could claim the title in the future.

▶ **More to explore**
Caesar, Julius • Ivan IV • Nicholas II • Peter the Great • Russia

Tshwane

▶ *see Pretoria.*

Tsunami

Natural disasters, both on land and under the ocean, may cause deadly ocean waves called tsunamis. By the time a tsunami reaches shore, it has gained tremendous size and power. Tsunamis can wipe out entire coastal villages or towns.

Earthquakes, landslides, or volcanic eruptions can trigger waves in a nearby ocean. These waves may travel for thousands of miles. They may move as fast as 500 miles (800 kilometers) an hour. As they approach a coastline, the waves move more slowly. They also rise, often to heights as great as 100 feet (30 meters). As the first huge wave nears

Did You Know?

Tsunami is a Japanese word. Tsunamis used to be called tidal waves, but they have nothing to do with tides.

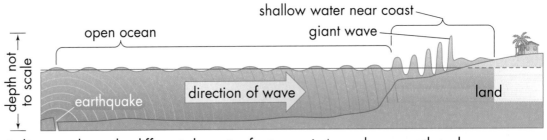

A diagram shows the different elements of a tsunami. An undersea earthquake causes waves to spread out in the ocean. As the waves approach a coast, they hit land under the water. This makes the waves much larger.

land, the coastal water often draws back dramatically. Then the tsunami hits the land.

Tsunamis cannot be stopped, but there are ways to defend against them. Scientists around the world watch for early signs of earthquakes. They also note unusual changes in ocean levels. With this information, scientists can warn people to leave areas that a tsunami might hit.

The Pacific Ocean is the site of many tsunamis, but tsunamis can form in the Atlantic and Indian oceans, too. A powerful earthquake struck beneath the Indian Ocean in December 2004. The earthquake set off tsunamis that hit about 10 countries. More than 200,000 people died.

▶ **More to explore**
Earthquake • Ocean

Tuberculosis

Tuberculosis, or TB, is a disease that usually affects the lungs. Tuberculosis used to be a leading cause of death in Europe and North America. Today tuberculosis is treatable.

Certain types of tiny living things called bacteria cause tuberculosis. One type of bacteria causes most cases of tuberculosis in humans. It infects the lungs. This may lead to coughing, chest pain, difficulty breathing, loss of energy, and weight loss. The person may even cough up blood. Infected people spread the disease to others when they cough or sneeze.

Another type of bacteria causes a less common form of tuberculosis. This form of tuberculosis may damage the bones and joints. Humans get it by

A doctor looks at the chest X-rays of patients infected with tuberculosis.

drinking milk from a cow infected with the bacteria. This form of tuberculosis can be prevented by pasteurizing milk, or heating it to kill the bacteria.

Tuberculosis spreads most easily in crowded places where living conditions are poor. In some countries people get something called a vaccine to protect them from tuberculosis. If people do get tuberculosis, doctors treat them with a medicine called an antibiotic. People given antibiotics have a good chance of recovering from the disease.

▶ **More to explore**
Bacteria • Disease, Human • Lung

Tubman, Harriet

Harriet Tubman

In the middle of the 1800s Harriet Tubman escaped from slavery in the southern United States. She then helped lead many other runaway slaves to freedom. She also served the Union during the American Civil War.

Harriet Tubman was born in about 1820 in Dorchester County, Maryland. She was one of 11 children of a slave family. Her name at first was Araminta Ross. She later changed her first name to Harriet, which was her mother's name.

In about 1844 Harriet married a free African American named John Tubman. In 1849, after hearing that she was to be sold, she escaped to Philadelphia, Pennsylvania, without her husband.

In Pennsylvania Tubman became a "conductor" for the Underground Railroad. The railroad was a secret network that helped escaped slaves to find their way to freedom. By 1857 she had freed hundreds of slaves, including her own parents. She said that she "never lost a passenger," even though slaveholders offered large rewards for her capture.

During the American Civil War, Tubman went to South Carolina with the Union Army. She served as a nurse and a scout. She even led raids against the Confederates.

After the Civil War Tubman settled in Auburn, New York, with her parents. There she worked for racial justice and also for women's rights. She believed that the two struggles were closely linked. In 1908 she opened a home for aged and poor African Americans. Harriet Tubman died in Auburn on March 10, 1913.

▶ **More to explore**
African Americans • American Civil War
• Slavery • Underground Railroad

Did You Know?

Tubman was called "the Moses of her people" because she led black people to freedom. (Moses led the Jewish people to freedom in ancient times.)

Tulip

Tulips are plants that bloom in early spring. The flowers are cup-shaped and very colorful. They are among the most popular garden flowers. There are about 4,000 varieties of tulip. They belong to the lily family.

Tulips first grew in south-central Asia. People brought the flowers to Europe in the 1500s and later to many different parts of the world. The Netherlands became the center of tulip production in the 1600s. It still is today.

Tulips normally grow from bulbs that are planted in autumn. Each bulb produces a plant each spring for a few years. A tulip plant has two or three thick, bluish green leaves. These are attached at the bottom of the stem. In most types of tulip each stem grows a single flower.

Tulip flowers occur in almost every color—white, yellow, pink, red, orange, purple, and even brown and black. The color is either solid or streaked. Streaked tulips get their streaks because of a harmless virus. The virus makes the top color disappear in some places. The flower's underlying white or yellow color then shows through.

Tulips surround the trunks of birch trees.

▶ More to explore

Flower • Lily • Netherlands, The

Tuna

Tuna are large fish that live in most parts of the world's oceans. They belong to the same family of fish as mackerel. Tuna is one of the most popular foods that comes from the sea. Most of the tuna that fishers catch is canned.

There are seven different species, or types, of tuna: bluefin, albacore, yellowfin, bigeye, blackfin, longtail, and southern bluefin. The skipjack tuna is related to these species, but it belongs to a separate group of fish.

A tuna has a long, rounded body. It is usually dark on top and silvery underneath. Some species have spots or stripes.

Many species of tuna are about 35 inches (90 centimeters) long. The bluefin tuna is the largest species. It can grow as long as 14 feet (4 meters) and weigh up to 1,800 pounds (800 kilograms).

Tuna travel in large groups called schools. Some species travel long distances. Tuna feed on other fish, including herring, menhaden, and mackerel.

The bluefin tuna is the largest type of tuna.

Some species also eat small, spineless animals such as squid. Some types of tuna return to the waters where they hatched to spawn, or produce eggs.

▶ **More to explore**
Fish

Tundra

Tundras are large, barren regions with no trees. In fact, the word tundra comes from the Finnish word *tunturia*, which means "treeless plain." Tundras lie between the permanent ice of the far north and the northern forests of North America, Europe, and Asia. They cover about 20 percent of Earth's surface.

Features

Tundras may be flat, hilly, or mountainous. Little plant life grows on the bare or rocky ground. Tundras in coastal areas tend to be foggy. Snow covers the world's tundras for more than six months of the year.

Types of Tundras

Arctic tundras lie in northern Europe, Russia, Alaska, Canada, and Greenland.

In these tundras the winter temperature may be as low as –25° F (–32° C). The summer temperature may rise only to 40° F (4° C). Because of these cold temperatures, Arctic tundras have a permanent layer of frozen soil, called permafrost. Some permafrost reaches as deep as 1,500 feet (456 meters).

Alpine tundras lie farther south than Arctic tundras. Alpine tundras are found in high mountains above the tree line. (The tree line is the highest place where trees can grow.) They have short, cool summers and less extreme winters than Arctic tundras. Alpine tundras do not have a layer of permafrost.

Life in a Tundra

Only low-growing plants, such as mosses and shrubs, can survive in tundras. Plantlike living things called lichens also grow there.

Tundra animals must be able to survive long, cold winters. Many birds live there in the summer, but few stay through the winter. Some common tundra animals

Reindeer graze on the Arctic tundra of Canada's Northwest Territories.

are reindeer, Arctic foxes, snowy owls, musk oxen, and polar bears.

Very few people live in tundras. Arctic peoples, including the Eskimo (Inuit), tend to live in places where hunting and fishing can provide enough food year-round.

Resources

The ground of many tundras contains coal, oil, iron ore, lead, or other resources. Many companies have set up mining operations in tundra regions. However, some people worry that mining and oil drilling endangers tundra plants and animals.

▶ More to explore
Eskimo • Lichen • Mining

Tunis

Population
(2007 estimate)
745,000

Tunis is the capital of Tunisia, a country in northern Africa. It is the largest city in Tunisia by far. Tunis lies near the coast of the Mediterranean Sea. A canal links it to a port on the sea.

Tunis is Tunisia's center of industry. Factories in the city make food products, cloth, clothing, and electronics. Many

The Grand Mosque of Tunis, Tunisia, is decorated with colorful tiles.

people in Tunis work in banking, tourism, or other service industries.

People called the Libyans founded Tunis in ancient times. Later, people called the Phoenicians built the city of Carthage nearby. Carthage became a great power. Tunis came under its rule. The Romans destroyed Tunis during a war with Carthage in 146 BC. They later rebuilt Tunis as a city of the Roman Empire.

Arabs captured Tunis in the AD 600s. The city later became the capital of a Muslim empire. In the 1200s Tunis was one of the leading cities in the Muslim world.

Tunis and the rest of Tunisia became part of the Turkish Ottoman Empire in 1574. France took control of Tunisia in 1881. In 1956 Tunisia became an independent country with Tunis as its capital.

▶ More to explore
Carthage • Tunisia

Tunisia

Tunisia is the smallest country in North Africa. In ancient times Tunisia was the site of the great city of Carthage. Today Tunisia's capital is Tunis.

Geography

Tunisia shares borders with Algeria and Libya. The Mediterranean Sea lies to the east and the north. Tunisia is only about 100 miles (160 kilometers) from Sicily, an island of Italy.

Mountain chains run through northern Tunisia. The country's largest river, the Majardah, flows through the north. The central part of Tunisia is a large plateau, or area of flat, raised land. There are shallow salt lakes farther south. The southern tip of Tunisia is a part of the Sahara Desert. The land there is sandy and rocky.

Northern Tunisia has mild, rainy winters and hot, dry summers. The south is warmer and drier.

Plants and Animals

Most of Tunisia's plants and animals are in the cooler northern region. The north has vineyards and forests of cork oak and evergreen oak. Thorny bushes and grasses grow farther south. The Sahara region in the far south has few plants.

Tunisia's animals include hyenas, wild boars, jackals, gazelles, and cobras. Scorpions live throughout the country.

People

Most of Tunisia's people have a mixture of Arab and Berber roots. (The Berbers were the first people in the region.) Most Tunisians call themselves Arabs. The main language is Arabic, but many people also speak French. Almost all the people are Muslims. More than half of all Tunisians live in cities and towns. Most people live near the Mediterranean coast.

Economy

Tourism and other services are key parts of Tunisia's economy. Manufacturing and mining are also important. The country's factories make processed foods, steel, chemicals, clothing, and leather goods. Tunisia also produces oil. Mines provide phosphates and iron. Tunisia uses the phosphates to make chemicals and fertilizers.

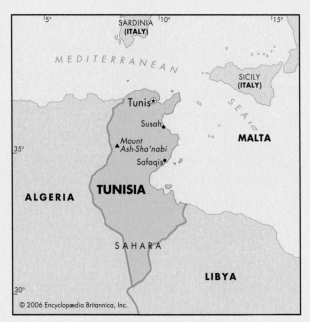

© 2006 Encyclopædia Britannica, Inc.

Tunisia is home to many ancient buildings, including Islamic buildings called *ribat*s. *Ribat*s served as both monasteries and fortresses.

Facts About
TUNISIA

Population
(2008 estimate)
10,325,000

Area
63,170 sq mi
(163,610 sq km)

Capital
Tunis

**Form of
government**
Republic

Major cities
Tunis, Safaqis,
Al-Arianah,
Ettadhamen,
Susah

Many Tunisians work in agriculture. Wheat and barley are the main food crops. Farmers also grow olives, tomatoes, sugar beets, citrus fruits, and dates. Sheep, goats, and cattle are the main livestock.

History

In ancient times Tunisia was a colony of the Phoenicians, a people from what is now Lebanon. In the 800s BC the Phoenicians founded the city of Carthage near what is now Tunis. By the 400s BC the city controlled trade in the western Mediterranean Sea. In the 200s and 100s BC Carthage fought Rome in a series of wars. The Romans destroyed Carthage in 146 BC and took over the land.

Muslim Arabs invaded the region in the AD 600s. Spain and the Ottoman Turks battled for control of the area in the 1500s. In 1574 the Turks defeated the Spanish and made Tunisia a part of the Ottoman Empire. As the Ottomans weakened in the late 1800s, France, Great Britain, and Italy tried to control the region. Tunisia became a territory of France in 1881. France allowed Tunisia's bey, or king, to stay on the throne, but the French held the real power.

Tunisia gained independence from France in 1956. The next year Tunisia ended its monarchy. The country's first president stayed in power until 1987. Tunisia's second president held power into the 21st century.

▶ **More to explore**
Carthage • Tunis

Turkey

Parts of Turkey are very mountainous.

The Republic of Turkey lies partly in Asia and partly in Europe. For centuries Turkey was the heart of two great empires—the Christian Byzantine Empire and the Islamic Ottoman Empire. Modern Turkey's capital is Ankara.

Geography

Most of Turkey is on a peninsula in southwestern Asia. A peninsula is a piece of land surrounded by water on three sides. The peninsula is known as Anatolia or Asia Minor. A small part of Turkey is in southeastern Europe. Narrow waterways and the Sea of Marmara separate the two parts of Turkey.

The Black Sea lies north of Turkey. Georgia, Armenia, and Iran are to the east. Iraq, Syria, and the Mediterranean Sea lie to the south. The Aegean Sea, Greece, and Bulgaria lie to the west.

The Asian part of Turkey has mountains and a central plateau, or raised flat area. The highest peak is Mount Ararat, which rises 16,853 feet (5,137 meters). The European part of Turkey is lower and flatter. The country's longest river, the Kizil, flows through the peninsula.

Most of Turkey has a dry climate with hot summers. Winters are cold in central Turkey and mild near the coasts. Earthquakes are common.

Plants and Animals

Grasslands cover much of the country. Pine, oak, cedar, juniper, and chestnut trees grow along the coast.

Deer, wild goats, bears, and lynx live near the Mediterranean coast. Gazelles and hyenas live in central and eastern Turkey. Wolves, jackals, badgers, and otters live throughout the country. Turkey's birds include buzzards, storks, vultures, and eagles.

People

Most of Turkey's people are Turks. They speak a language called Turkish. Most of the rest of the people are Kurds. They live in eastern Turkey and have their own language. Almost all the people of Turkey follow Islam.

More than half of the population lives in cities and towns. Turkey's largest city is Istanbul.

Economy

Services and manufacturing are the main parts of Turkey's economy. Services include communications, transportation, and tourism. Manufacturers produce fabrics, clothing, processed foods, iron and steel, chemicals, cars, and electronics. Turkey's land provides oil, coal, copper, and other minerals.

The Hagia Sophia in Istanbul, Turkey, has been a Christian church and a Muslim mosque. Now it is a museum.

Many Turks are farmers. Wheat, sugar beets, citrus fruits, cotton, olives, tobacco, and figs are important crops. Sheep, cattle, and goats are the main livestock.

History

Humans have lived in the Asian part of Turkey, called Anatolia, since at least 7000 BC. The Hittite people invaded in about 2000 BC. Greeks and Persians later fought over the land. Romans took over Anatolia by about 30 BC.

Byzantine Empire

Under the Roman Empire, Anatolia was at peace. In AD 395 the Roman Empire was divided into western and eastern parts. The eastern part became known as the Byzantine Empire. Its capital was the city of Constantinople (now called Istanbul). Christianity was the main religion of the Byzantine Empire.

The Seljuk Turks invaded Anatolia beginning in the 1040s. The Seljuk Turks were Muslims from central Asia. In 1071 they defeated the Byzantine army. During the next 200 years the Christians of Europe fought the Turks in a series of wars known as the Crusades.

Ottoman Empire

In the late 1200s a new group of Turks gained power in Anatolia. They founded the great Ottoman Empire. In 1453 the Ottoman Turks captured Constantinople. They renamed the city Istanbul and made it their capital.

TIMELINE

about 2000 BC	about 30 BC	AD 395	1071	1300	1923	1983
Hittites invade Anatolia.		Anatolia becomes part of the Byzantine Empire.		The Ottoman Turks gain power.		Kurds begin fighting the Turkish government.
	Romans take control of Anatolia.		The Seljuk Turks defeat the Byzantines.		The Republic of Turkey is formed.	

By the mid-1500s the Ottoman Empire stretched across North Africa, the Middle East, and southeastern Europe. The empire then grew weaker. It collapsed at the end of World War I in 1918.

Turkey Under Atatürk

After the war many Turks were angry at the Ottoman government, which had lost much of the empire's land. A military leader named Mustafa Kemal formed a separate government. In 1923 he founded the new country of Turkey. The city of Ankara became the new capital. Kemal became Turkey's first president.

Kemal ruled with strong powers. He soon took the name Atatürk, which is Turkish for "father of the Turks." Atatürk wanted to make Turkey a more modern country. He closed Islamic schools and courts. He banned traditional clothes such as the fez, a type of Turkish hat. He also gave women the right to vote. Atatürk died in 1938.

Turkey After Atatürk

In 1960 and 1980 the military took over Turkey's government. In 1997 the military forced the prime minister to step down. Each time Turkey returned to democracy.

Beginning in the 1950s Turkey disagreed with Greece over control of the island of Cyprus. Turkish forces invaded northern Cyprus in 1974. Turkey supported the Turks of Cyprus when they formed a separate country in 1983.

Modern Turkey has also faced a long rebellion by Kurds in the east. The Kurds fought the Turkish government from the 1980s into the 21st century.

▶ **More to explore**
Ankara • Byzantine Empire • Cyprus • Islam • Istanbul • Kurd • Ottoman Empire

Facts About TURKEY

Population
(2008 estimate)
71,002,000

Area
299,158 sq mi
(744,815 sq km)

Capital
Ankara

Form of government
Republic

Major cities
Istanbul, Ankara, Izmir, Bursa, Adana

Turkey

Two male common turkeys in the wild display their feathers.

Turkeys are large birds. They are found in the wild and they are also raised for food. The two species, or types, of turkey are the common turkey and the ocellated turkey.

The common turkey prefers places with mild temperatures. It usually has black feathers mixed with a shiny green or bronze color. The head and neck are featherless, bumpy, and bright red. Males have a piece of red skin growing from the forehead. Male turkeys often make a gobbling sound while females make a clicking noise.

Some common turkeys live in the wild. They are found in parts of Mexico and the United States. Wild turkeys prefer forests and swamps. Males weigh about 22 pounds (10 kilograms), but females are much smaller. Wild turkeys can fly, but only for short distances.

Many common turkeys are kept on farms and raised for food. These turkeys are usually heavier, and they cannot fly. Their feathers are usually white.

The ocellated turkey is found in Central America. It is much smaller than the common turkey. It has a blue head and neck with reddish yellow bumps. Its tail feathers are tipped with blue and gold, somewhat like a peacock. The ocellated turkey is not raised for food.

(Left) Many turkeys are raised for their meat; (right) ocellated turkeys live only in the wild.

Turkmenistan

A vendor sells dried fruits and nuts at a market in Turkmenistan.

Turkmenistan is a desert country in central Asia. The capital is Ashgabat.

Turkmenistan is on the southeastern coast of the Caspian Sea. It shares borders with Kazakhstan, Uzbekistan, Afghanistan, and Iran.

The sandy Karakum Desert covers most of the land. Southern Turkmenistan has some mountains and hills. Turkmenistan

has a very dry climate with hot summers and cold winters.

Grasses and shrubs grow in the dry areas. Fig and nut trees grow near the mountains. Foxes, wildcats, cobras, lizards, and gazelles live in the desert. Leopards and porcupines live in the hills.

Turkmenistan is named after its main group of people, the Turkmen. The country also has some Uzbeks, Russians, and Kazakhs. Most of the Turkmen are Muslims. The people live mainly in southern oases (desert areas with a water supply) and along the rivers in the east.

The economy of Turkmenistan depends on agriculture and the production of natural gas and oil. Farming is possible with the help of irrigation, or artificial watering systems. The main crops are cotton and grain. People also raise sheep and use their wool to make carpets. Factories produce metals, machinery, chemicals, and fabrics.

The Parthian Empire of Iran ruled the region in ancient times. Turkmen nomads, or wanderers, entered the area by AD 1100. Russia conquered the region by 1881. In 1925 Turkmenistan became part of the Soviet Union. Turkmenistan gained independence in 1991.

▶ **More to explore**
Ashgabat

© 2006 Encyclopædia Britannica, Inc.

Facts About TURKMENISTAN

Population
(2008 estimate)
5,180,000

Area
188,500 sq mi
(488,100 sq km)

Capital
Ashgabat

Form of government
Republic

Major cities
Ashgabat, Turkmenabat, Dashhowuz, Mary, Balkanabat

Turner, Nat

THE
CONFESSIONS
OF
NAT TURNER,
THE LEADER
OF
THE LATE INSURRECTION
IN SOUTHAMPTON, VA.
AS FULLY AND VOLUNTARILY MADE TO
THOMAS R. GRAY,
In the prison where he was confined, and acknowledged by him to be such,
when read before the Court of Southampton: with the
certificate, under seal of the Court convened at
Jerusalem, Nov. 5, 1831, for his trial.
ALSO,
AN AUTHENTIC ACCOUNT
OF THE
WHOLE INSURRECTION,
WITH
Lists of the Whites who were Murdered,
AND OF THE
Negroes brought before the Court of Southampton,
and there sentenced, &c.

RICHMOND:
PUBLISHED BY THOMAS R. GRAY.
T. W. WHITE, PRINTER.
1832.

An account of Nat Turner's slave rebellion was published in 1832.

In the United States before the American Civil War, many slaves escaped to freedom. Others rebelled with violence against their owners. A slave named Nat Turner led one of the bloodiest slave revolts in U.S. history. Southern states reacted to Turner's revolt by passing laws that made the lives of slaves even more difficult.

Early Life
Nat Turner was born on October 2, 1800, on a farm in Virginia. He had several owners. In 1831 he joined the household of a man named Travis.

Unlike most slaves, Turner learned to read and write. He also learned about the Christian religion. He came to believe that God had chosen him to free all slaves.

Revolt
On August 21, 1831, Turner and seven other slaves killed everyone in the Travis family. In the next two days, Turner picked up about 75 followers. They killed about 60 white people.

Then about 3,000 whites rose up to stop the revolt. Whites killed most of Turner's men. Whites captured Turner, put him on trial, and put him to death on November 11, 1831.

Turner's revolt frightened Southern whites. They blamed his rebellious spirit on his education, so they tried to stop slaves from learning to read and write. They also tried to stop slaves from gathering in groups.

▶ **More to explore**
Slavery

Turtle

A turtle is a reptile that has a shell covering its body. Turtles are known for moving very slowly. There are about 250 species, or types, of turtle.

Turtles are found in most parts of the world. Most live in freshwater ponds, lakes, or rivers. Others live in the ocean or on land. Some turtles live in forests or even in the desert. Land turtles are often called tortoises. Some water turtles are known as terrapins.

A desert tortoise creeps among wildflowers in the U.S. state of California.

Turtles are all different sizes. The smallest turtles are less than 4 inches (10 centimeters) long. In contrast, the Atlantic leatherback turtle can be more than 7 feet (2 meters) long. It can weigh more than 1,500 pounds (680 kilograms).

Turtles have sturdy legs with short feet and claws on the toes. Sea turtles have flippers instead of front feet. A turtle's shell is made of bone. It is usually very hard and strong. Most turtles can tuck the head, legs, and tail inside the shell for protection from enemies. Snapping turtles cannot do this, but they have a powerful bite for protection.

Turtles eat worms, snails, insects, jellyfish, and shellfish. Many tortoises eat only plants. Turtles can store food in the form of fat. Some turtles can store water, too. They can live for days or even weeks without having anything to eat or drink.

All turtles lay their eggs on land. The female digs a hole and lays her eggs in it. The temperature in the nest usually affects the sex of the baby turtles.

Warmer temperatures generally produce females, while cooler temperatures produce males.

Turtles live longer than most other animals. Some species can live more than 100 years.

▶ **More to explore**
Reptile

Tuscarora

The Tuscarora are Native Americans of New York State and Ontario, Canada. In the 1700s they became the sixth tribe to join the group called the Iroquois Confederacy.

The Tuscarora lived in round homes made from poles covered with bark. Later they also lived in homes called longhouses, which were large enough for

A Tuscarora dancer performs at the New York State Fair in Geddes, New York.

several families. The Tuscarora grew corn, gourds, beans, and apples. They also hunted and gathered wild plants.

By the early 1700s British colonists had moved into Tuscarora territory. At that time the Tuscarora lived in North Carolina and Virginia. The settlers mistreated the tribe. They kidnapped Tuscarora men, women, and children and sold them as slaves. They also took the tribe's lands without payment.

The Tuscarora fought back in 1711 by attacking several British settlements. The attacks started a war. At least 1,000 Tuscarora were killed in the fighting. The Tuscarora who survived fled north to New York. There, in 1722, they joined the Iroquois Confederacy.

After the American Revolution (1775–83) many Tuscarora moved to new lands near Lewiston, New York. That area later became the Tuscarora Reservation. Some Tuscarora moved to lands along the Grand River in what is now Ontario. That area is now the Six Nations Reserve. At the end of the 20th century nearly 2,500 Tuscarora lived in the United States. More than 1,900 others lived in Canada.

▶ **More to explore**
Iroquois • Native Americans

Did You Know?

Most of the Tuscarora were on the side of the colonists during the American Revolution.

A poster from World War II shows an African American airman.

Tuskegee Airmen

The Tuskegee Airmen were the first group of African Americans to fly warplanes for the U.S. military. They served during World War II. At that time, during the 1940s, African Americans had fewer rights than whites had. The Tuskegee Airmen did their jobs as well as any white pilots. After seeing how well the airmen did, other African Americans pushed harder for equal rights.

Before the United States entered World War II, the National Association for the Advancement of Colored People (NAACP) asked the U.S. government to allow African Americans to fly warplanes. The military was then segregated, or separated by race. Because of this, the U.S. Army started a training program for African Americans only.

The airmen got their training in Alabama at the Tuskegee Army Air Field and at an African American college called Tuskegee Institute. The first Tuskegee Airmen graduated in 1942. Eventually 992 pilots graduated from the training program.

The Tuskegee Airmen served in Europe and North Africa. They flew small airplanes that protected bigger airplanes that dropped bombs on enemy targets. The airmen never allowed an enemy airplane to shoot down a U.S. bomber.

In 1948, three years after World War II ended, President Harry S. Truman ended racial segregation in the military. After that African Americans served alongside whites.

▶ **More to explore**
African Americans • National Association for the Advancement of Colored People • World War II

Tutankhamen

Tutankhamen was a pharaoh, or king, of ancient Egypt in the 1300s BC. He became pharaoh when he was still a child. He is famous today because of the many treasures found inside his tomb, or grave.

Life
Tutankhamen married while very young. His wife was the daughter of another pharaoh named Akhenaton. Akhenaton had tried to change the religion of ancient Egypt. He wanted Egyptians to have one god only, instead of many gods. Tutankhamen brought back the old religion with its many gods. He died at about age 18.

Tomb and Treasures
Workers dug Tutankhamen's tomb into a hillside in southern Egypt. The place is

called the Valley of the Kings. (By Tutankhamen's time, Egyptians had stopped burying pharaohs in pyramids.)

Thousands of years ago, robbers broke into the tombs of other pharaohs in the Valley of the Kings. They stole many treasures from the tombs. The robbers missed Tutankhamen's tomb because rubble from another tomb covered up the entrance.

In 1922 Howard Carter, a British archaeologist, found Tutankhamen's tomb and opened it. (An archaeologist is a scientist who studies things that people made in the past.) Carter found Tutankhamen's mummy, or preserved body, within a nest of three coffins. The inner coffin was solid gold. A gold mask with the face of the pharaoh covered the mummy's head. The tomb also con-

Tutankhamen's tomb was opened in 1922. One of the most spectacular objects in the tomb was a gold mask. It covered the head of the king's mummy.

tained furniture, statues, clothes, a chariot, weapons, staffs, and various other objects. The government of Egypt now owns these treasures.

▶ **More to explore**
Egypt, Ancient • Mummy • Pharaoh

Tutu, Desmond

Desmond Tutu is a religious leader in South Africa. His protests helped to bring an end to South Africa's apartheid laws. Apartheid was a system that kept blacks separate from whites. In 1984 Tutu received the Nobel peace prize for his work.

Early Life

Desmond Mpilo Tutu was born on October 7, 1931, in Klerksdorp, South Africa. His father was a schoolteacher. Tutu graduated from the University of South Africa in 1954.

Desmond Tutu

Tutu taught school for three years. Then he went back to college to study religion. In 1961 he became a priest in the Anglican church. He then taught religion in South Africa and Lesotho (another country in southern Africa).

Career

Between 1972 and 1975 Tutu worked in Great Britain for a Christian group called the World Council of Churches. Then he returned to Africa to serve the Anglican church.

Between 1978 and 1985 Tutu led the South African Council of Churches. During this time he frequently made nonviolent protests against apartheid laws. The apartheid system made life hard for blacks. They did not have the same rights as whites.

In 1986 Tutu became archbishop of Cape Town, South Africa. This made him the leader of South Africa's 1.6-million-member Anglican church. He was the first black to hold this job. In 1988 Tutu also became chancellor (president) of the University of the Western Cape in Bellville, South Africa. He continued to protest against apartheid.

Apartheid finally ended in the early 1990s. In 1995 Tutu led a committee that investigated the crimes of apartheid. He retired as archbishop in 1996, but he continued to teach.

▶ **More to explore**
Apartheid • South Africa

Tuvalu

A traditional hut sits among palm trees on Funafuti Atoll in Tuvalu.

The country of Tuvalu is made up of nine small island groups in the Pacific Ocean. Tuvalu's capital is Vaiaku, on the island group called Funafuti Atoll.

Geography

Tuvalu is in Polynesia, a part of the large region called Oceania. Tuvalu's islands are made of coral. Five of the island groups are atolls. Atolls are groups of islets (small islands) that surround a pool of water. Most of Tuvalu's land is

only about 15 feet (4.5 meters) above sea level. There are no rivers. Tuvalu's climate is hot and rainy.

Plants and Animals

Coconut palms, screw pines, ferns, and grasses grow on the islands. Wildlife includes Polynesian rats, lizards, and turtles. Octopuses, crustaceans, and many fish live in Tuvalu's waters.

People

Almost all the people are Polynesians. Most people speak a language called Tuvaluan. English is also common. Most people are Christians. Nearly half of the population lives on Funafuti Atoll.

Economy

Most people work in agriculture and fishing. Crops include coconuts, tropical fruit, and sweet potatoes. Many people leave the country to find work. Tuvalu's government sells its stamps to stamp collectors around the world. Tuvalu also sells the use of its Internet name, ".tv."

History

The first settlers in Tuvalu came from the islands of Samoa in about the AD 1300s. In 1892 Great Britain took over Tuvalu, which was then called the Ellice Islands. In 1916 Britain joined the Ellice Islands with the Gilbert Islands (now the country of Kiribati). The Ellice Islands gained independence as Tuvalu in 1978.

▶ **More to explore**
Coral • Funafuti Atoll • Oceania

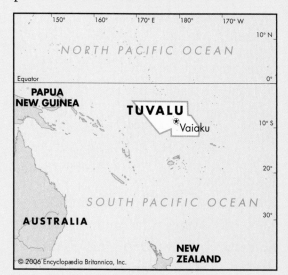

Facts About TUVALU

Population (2008 estimate) 9,600

Area 10 sq mi (26 sq km)

Capital Vaiaku, on Funafuti Atoll

Form of government Constitutional monarchy

Major town Fongafale islet

Twain, Mark

The U.S. author Mark Twain wrote stories of youthful adventures. His stories are treasured by readers around the world. He created Tom Sawyer, Huck Finn, and other memorable characters.

Twain's real name was Samuel Langhorne Clemens. Mark Twain was the name he used as a writer. He was born on November 30, 1835, in the small town of Florida, Missouri. When he was 4 years old he moved with his family to Hannibal, Missouri, on the Mississippi River.

In 1847 Samuel's father died. From then on Samuel had to help support the family. At age 13 he started working with a local printer. Later he worked as a printer for newspapers in Saint Louis, Missouri; New York City; and Philadelphia, Pennsylvania. In the late 1850s

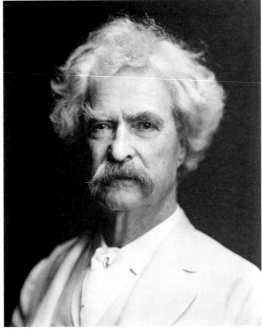

Mark Twain

and early 1860s he piloted steamboats on the Mississippi.

Clemens also wrote humorous stories for newspapers. In the 1860s he started writing under the name Mark Twain. In 1865 he published a story called "The Celebrated Jumping Frog of Calaveras County." It made him famous.

In the 1870s Twain settled with his family in Hartford, Connecticut. There he wrote his most famous books. He used his experiences growing up on the Mississippi River to write many of his stories. His novel *The Adventures of Tom Sawyer* (1876) is a story about a boy and his friends in a small river town. *The Adventures of Huckleberry Finn* (1884) tells of a boy's adventures as he floats down the Mississippi on a raft. *Huckleberry Finn* was his best book.

Late in life Twain lived mainly in Europe with his family. He died in Redding, Connecticut, on April 21, 1910.

Tyler, John

The 10th president of the United States, John Tyler did not win a presidential election. He took office after the death of President William Henry Harrison in 1841.

Early Life

John Tyler was born on March 29, 1790, at Greenway, his family's plantation near Richmond, Virginia. He was the son of Mary Armistead and John

John Tyler was the 10th president of the United States.

Tyler, Sr., a judge and former governor of Virginia.

After graduating from the College of William and Mary in 1807, Tyler became a lawyer at age 19. He married Letitia Christian in 1813. The couple had eight children.

Political Career

Tyler entered the Virginia legislature in 1811. In 1816 he was elected to the U.S. House of Representatives. He served again in the Virginia legislature before becoming governor of Virginia in 1825. Two years later he was elected to the U.S. Senate, where he served until 1836.

Although Tyler was a Democrat, he disagreed with Democratic president Andrew Jackson. He and many Southern Democrats joined the Whig Party. In 1840 the Whigs chose Tyler to run for vice president under Harrison. Harrison and Tyler won the election.

Presidency

President Harrison died just one month after taking office. He was the first president to die in office, and the Constitution did not say whether the vice president should become president or just act as president. Tyler decided that he was president.

TIMELINE

Tyler is born near Richmond, Virginia.

Tyler is elected vice president under William Henry Harrison.

Tyler leaves office.

Tyler dies in Richmond, Virginia.

| March 29, 1790 | 1825 | 1840 | 1841 | 1845 | 1861 | January 18, 1862 |

Tyler becomes governor of Virginia.

Tyler becomes president after Harrison dies.

Tyler wins a seat in the Confederate Congress.

Neither the Whigs nor the Democrats supported Tyler. Still, he led Congress to reorganize the Navy and to establish the Weather Bureau. He ended an expensive war against the Seminole people in Florida. He also helped to stop a rebellion against the state government of Rhode Island in 1842. Finally, Tyler got Congress to agree to take over the Republic of Texas.

Tyler's wife died in 1842. In 1844 Tyler married Julia Gardiner. They had seven children.

Later Years

For the presidential election of 1844 Tyler created his own political party, but he soon dropped out of the race. He left office in 1845.

Tyler was a slave owner, but before the American Civil War (1861–65) he wanted to keep the Union together. When the war began, however, he supported the South and was elected to the Confederate House of Representatives. Before taking office, he died in Richmond on January 18, 1862.

▶ **More to explore**
Confederate States of America
• Harrison, William Henry • Jackson, Andrew • United States

Typhoid Fever

Typhoid fever is a serious disease. It is rare in wealthy countries but common in poor ones. People with the disease usually have a high fever for many days. Other symptoms, or signs, of typhoid fever include headache, stomach pain, and weakness. A rash of rosy spots also may appear on the body.

Tiny living things called bacteria cause typhoid fever. The type of bacteria that causes the disease lives only in humans. It travels in the blood and attacks the intestines. It passes from person to person through water or food.

Typhoid fever may be prevented by keeping water supplies clean. Washing the hands before preparing food is important, too. People also may get a typhoid fever vaccine (a substance that prevents the disease) from a doctor or a nurse. People who do get the disease need to be treated with drugs called antibiotics. People who are not treated may die.

In the early 1900s a cook called Mary Mallon spread typhoid fever to at least 51 people in the United States. She carried the bacteria but did not get the disease. She passed the bacteria to people through food that she prepared. Mallon's actions earned her the nickname Typhoid Mary.

▶ **More to explore**
Bacteria • Disease, Human

Typhus

Typhus is the name of several diseases caused by tiny living things called bacteria. The symptoms of typhus include headache, fever, and rash. Lice, fleas, mites, and ticks carry the types of bacteria that cause typhus. These bloodsuckers pass the bacteria to humans.

To prevent typhus, people should keep lice, fleas, mites, and ticks from getting on their skin. People also can get a vaccine, or substance that prevents the disease. If a person does get typhus, drugs called antibiotics can cure it.

▶ **More to explore**
Disease, Human

Tyrannosaurus Rex

Tyrannosaurus rex, or *T. rex*, was one of the largest and most ferocious predators ever to walk on Earth. The name *Tyrannosaurus rex* means "king of the tyrant lizards." *T. rex* was just one of the group of dinosaurs called tyrannosaurs. The tyrannosaurs were theropods, or meat-eating dinosaurs that walked on their two back legs.

When and Where *Tyrannosaurus rex* Lived

T. rex lived about 80 to 65 million years ago. Fossil remains of *T. rex* have been found in the United States, Canada, and Asia. Scientists believe that *T. rex* lived in forests and in forest clearings.

Physical Features

T. rex could reach a length of 42 feet (13 meters) and weighed up to 8 tons. Its huge head could reach 5 feet (1.5 meters) in length, and its skull alone weighed up to 600 pounds (270 kilograms). Its eyes allowed it to see forward and to the sides. *T. rex* had about 60 teeth with sawlike edges. It had muscular back legs, each with three clawed toes. *T. rex*'s front legs were tiny but very strong. Its tail was held off the ground.

Behavior

T. rex preyed on plant-eating dinosaurs. It most likely lunged out from behind trees in surprise attacks. It also may have hunted in packs to bring down much larger dinosaurs. Scientists estimate that *T. rex* could run 20 miles per hour (32 kilometers per hour) for short distances. *T. rex* also may have been a scavenger, feeding upon dead animals.

▶ **More to explore**
Dinosaur

Tyrannosaurus rex

DATE DUE			